KAFFE FASSETT'S
Quilts in Morocco

20 designs from Rowan for patchwork and quilting

featuring

Liza Prior Lucy • Pauline Smith

Ruth Eglinton • Julie Stockler

Judy Baldwin • Corienne Kramer

Sally Davis • Brandon Mably

A ROWAN PUBLICATION

The Taunton Press

The Taunton Press
Inspiration for hands-on living®

The Taunton Press, Inc., 63 South Main Street,
PO Box 5506, Newtown, CT 06470-5506
email: tp@taunton.com

First published in Great Britain in 2014 by
Rowan
Green Lane Mill
Holmfirth
West Yorkshire
England HD9 2DX

Patchwork designs	Kaffe Fassett, Liza Prior Lucy, Pauline Smith, Brandon Mably, Judy Baldwin, Julie Stockler Sally Davis, Corienne Kramer, Ruth Eglinton
Art direction/styling	Kaffe Fassett
Editor	Pauline Smith
Technical editor	Ruth Eglinton
Designer	Anne Wilson
Location photography	Debbie Patterson
Additional location photography	Brandon Mably: 4 above; 5; 6 above and below; 7 top row left and right, middle row centre and right, bottom row left and right; 8 left and right; 9; 13; 33 right; 49 above right; 87
Stills photography	Dave Tolson
Illustrations	Ruth Eglinton
Quilters	Judy Irish, Pauline Smith

Publishing consultant Susan Berry

Library of Congress Cataloging-in-Publication Data in
progress

ISBN 978-1-62710-743-3

Color reproduction by XY Digital Ltd, UK
Printed by KHL Printing Co Pte Ltd, Singapore

Page 1: The lush scarlets and magentas of
the *Cayenne* quilt are radiant in the exotically
furnished cobalt room at Café Fez.
Right: Kaffe's *Shuttle* quilt (detail) under the
leg of a table in the beautifully restored Raid
Idrissy in Fez (where they stayed during the
shoot).

Contents

Welcome to Fez

After shooting my last three books in the colourful, distinctly different but very definitely European worlds of Cornwall, Bulgaria and the south of France, our shoot for this book in the Moroccan hill-top city, Fez, plunged us into the kaleidoscopic world of medieval Islam. When growing up on the coast of California I had heard this city spoken of with reverence; travelling there years later, I found it very much the way it had been described to me. I felt it would make a flavourful, very different location for this collection on quilts.

The walled city of Fez, with its winding streets and bustling markets, was challenging at first. But, thanks to our young helper, Mustapha Harouni, we were able to explore its delights, wandering deep into the Medina without fear of getting lost in its maze of narrow alleyways with few street signs.

The hotel in which we stayed, the Raid Idrissy, is a beautifully restored, traditional 18th-century house, its rooms are arranged on four floors that look down into a central atrium with its typical, elaborately patterned mosaic and tiled floor. The huge wooden doors to the main ground floor rooms are intricately carved and beautifully painted in ochre and rust tones.

We ate in the Raid's now famous Ruined Garden restaurant – housed in the lush garden that blooms in the ruins of the next-door house. Its beautiful crumbling tiled floor is almost obscured by the plants that sprout vigorously from every kind of container: ancient clay vessels, baskets and even plastic buckets.

We were able to shoot several quilts in this handsome hotel and several more in its neighbouring hotel up the same winding street. At Le Jardin des

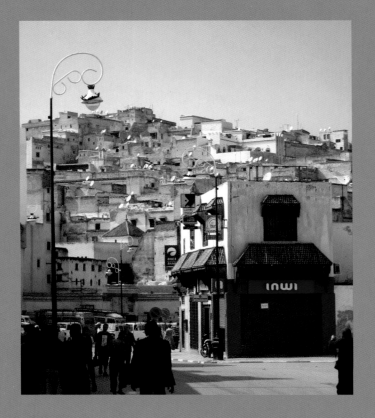

Biehn Raid, a deliciously decorated hotel founded and run by two antique dealers from Paris: Michel Biehn and his son, Paul, we were given free rein to explore and shoot our quilts in the garden, café and exotically decorated rooms of the Raid. The painted woodwork, toned walls and tiled surfaces made this a rich background for our quilts.

While in Fez, we had the good fortune to meet David Amster, head of the Arabic Language Institute in Fez (ALIF). He is an enthusiast of Islamic buildings, which are showcased on his architectural website: Ahouseinfez.com. David dwells in an 18th-century house that he is very sensitively restoring, and in which we were allowed to photograph. It was amazing to be in a stripped-back, mostly empty space that had been painstakingly constructed by craftsmen of old in their traditional style, so that every floor and half the

walls were tiled. The doors and window surrounds, and even the wooden ceiling, were all carved and painted. Once more, our quilts came to life in this handsome setting.

As you wander the markets in this mysterious old city, you clearly see that these ancient traditional crafts are still alive and well. We came across so many open workshops where we experienced the sight and sound of today's craftsmen at work, including weaving, carving, metal working, making pottery and painting furniture. Laden donkeys carry goods though crowded streets lined with stalls offering an eclectic mix of pottery, richly colored scarves, shoes, fruit, vegetables and spices. Street cafés, decorated with bright tablecloths, serving aromatic mint leaf tea and good Moroccan food, abound.

Though the predominant colour of Fez is the light adobe clay of the high walls that line the streets, there are also mosaic fountains, colourful market goods and a constant parade of brightly coloured robes of women shoppers, making Fez a rich tapestry to behold. In short, the perfect complement to our detailed highly coloured quilts!

the fabrics

Here is a selection of the current fabrics by Kaffe (code indicator GP), Philip Jacobs (code indicator PJ) and Brandon Mably (code indicator BM) grouped into colour palettes. Many of the fabrics in the selection have been used in the collection of quilts in this book, but there are plenty of others in the range for you to choose from when making your quilts.

◄ Blues

PJ54 Cactus Dahlia (blue)
BM22 Dancing Paisley (regal)
GP136 Uzbekistan (blue)
BM15 Rings (robin's egg)
GP137 Ribbon Stripe (blue)
PJ62 Brocade Peony (blue)
PJ60 Joy (blue)
GP135 Surrey (cobalt)
BM39 Crackle (blue)

Greens ►

PJ54 Cactus Dahlia (green)
WCS Caterpillar Stripe (blue)
GP136 Uzbekistan (green)
PJ64 Lavinia (green)
PJ62 Brocade Peony (green)
BM40 Jolly (grey)
BM39 Crackle (grey)
WCS Caterpillar Stripe (sprout)
PJ61 Bouffant (green)

◄ Pastels

PJ60 Joy (yellow)
GP135 Surrey (turquoise)
PJ62 Brocade Peony (yellow)
BM37 Mad Plaid (pastel)
GP137 Ribbon Stripe (yellow)
GP136 Uzbekistan (yellow)
GP134 Flame Stripe (yellow)
BM43 Zig Zag (pink)
PJ51 Brassica (yellow)

Reds ►

GP133 Belle Epoch (red)
PJ60 Joy (pink)
BM43 ZigZag (warm)
GP136 Uzbekistan (red)
GP128 Chard (hot)
GP134 Flame Stripe (red)
GP137 Ribbon Stripe (red)
PJ61 Bouffant (red)
PJ62 Brocade Peony (red)

Note: If you need to make a fabric substitution, it is more important to go by the combined effect of the colour and pattern together, rather than looking for an exact colour match, say, to the background colour alone.

Flying Geese
by Kaffe Fassett

My *Flying Geese* quilt reflects the shapes in a typical old carpet in the Fez market. The geometric elements (Brandon's Zig Zag fabric on the border) work so well with the intricate details of the traditional Moroccan architecture.

Strata
by Kaffe Fassett

My *Strata* quilt, made from all the Zig Zag and Jupiter Stripe
fabrics in our collection, blends beautifully with the ancient
elegance of this room and on the shoulder of a boldly dressed
doorman at Café Fez.

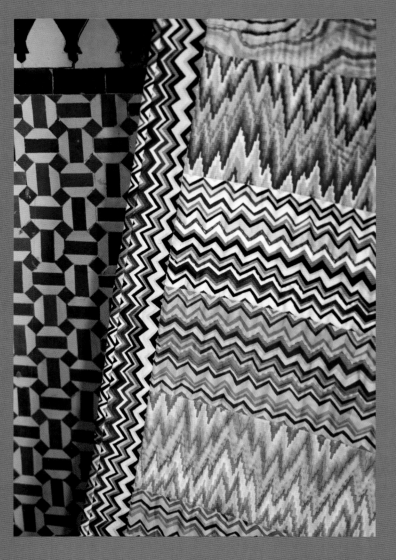

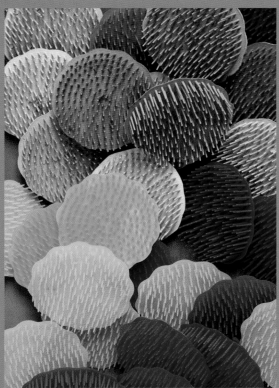

Sunny Snowballs
by Kaffe Fassett

The Fez fruit market makes the perfect setting for my *Sunny Snowball* quilt. I particularly love the brilliant colours on these plastic combs that we spotted on a street stall.

Paisley Columns
by Kaffe Fassett

Paisley Columns shows our new Paisley print, Belle Epoch, to advantage under an earthy portrait in the Café Fez. A carved and painted door is the perfect shape for the flow of this quilt.

18

Shuttles
by Kaffe Fassett

My *Shuttles* quilt was inspired by an early
American quilt I found in a book. Its jolly,
optimistic palette is gorgeously mirrored in
the rack of shoes in the market. Lime Millefiore
makes a spicy print to line my quilt.

Library
by Kaffe Fassett

Loving books, and the way they look on shelves, this is an idea of mine that's been waiting to happen for years. I used our Shot Cottons and Ombre stripe fabrics to create *trompe l'oeil* shelves that remind me how my grandmother used to arrange her books by the colour of their spines. How perfect to show it off on the old painted door in our Raid!

Water Garden
by Kaffe Fassett

This icy blue corner of the
Café Fez made the colours in
my *Water Garden* quilt ping
to life. The Ombre sashing
looking particularly juicy.

Pastel Blush
by Kaffe Fassett

Pastel Blush, with its high colours, found a nice home on the softly toned walls and bright cushion in Café Fez's garden.

Rouge
by Kaffe Fassett

The *Rouge* quilt arrived from a simple process of taking every bright red and pink fabric in the current collection and putting them together in basic squares with an Ombre border. In this cool green lattice room it glows like a shower of bougainvillea blooms. My pink Hawaiian shirt isn't bad in this context either! Philip Jacobs' Brocade Peony print is just perfect for the backing.

Even Weave
by Liza Prior Lucy

Another antique Moroccan painted door makes a theatrical show of the *Even Weave* quilt by Liza Prior Lucy. Her cool choice of blue and lime-green Indian woven stripe is perfect for this easy-to-make quilt.

Spice Mountain
by Liza Prior Lucy

Liza Prior Lucy's *Spice Mountain* is a great subject matter for a quilt with these traditional blocks. It reflects the wonderful sacks of aromatic spices found in the Fez Medina.

Blue Morocco (overleaf)
by Liza Prior Lucy

This quilt settles into the ancient interior as if it were made in the same era. The mosaic floor, carved doors and old brass are perfectly in tune with the elegant ripple of colour of the rhythmic repeated pattern.

Fountain
by Ruth Eglinton

The watery palette of Ruth Eglinton's *Fountain* quilt is shown well on this turquoise ironwork window. My favorite new thing in Fez is this gigantic tiled mural that amusingly refers to the small-scale mosaics round the old fountains of Fez.

Carnaby
by Brandon Mably

Brandon Mably's very geometric quilt disappointed me until I saw how it reflected so amazingly the intricate patterns on the tiled floor in our Raid. It flows through the beautifully decorated old pots at the Café Fez.

Diamond Delight
by Sally Davis

Diamond Delight by Sally Davis glows with all the colours of the Medina. The blue Millefiore backing is as intricate as the carefully painted frames on the window of our Raid.

Teapots
by Pauline Smith

The jaunty colours of the restaurant at Café Fez made a perfect framework for Pauline Smith's *Teapots* quilt. The scarlet tablecloths and sky blue chairs are echoed in the gypsy patterns and tones of her quilt.

Mediterranean Hexagons
by Judy Baldwin

In my blue shirt I look like a block that escaped from Judy Baldwin's *Mediterranean Hexagons* quilt. The soft blue-green woodwork at Café Fez sets off the jewel blues to perfection.

Mellow Vintage
by Pauline Smith

The dusty palette of Pauline Smith's *Mellow Vintage* quilt found a good home amongst this collection of terracotta jars. Scarves in the market echo the bright notes in her piece.

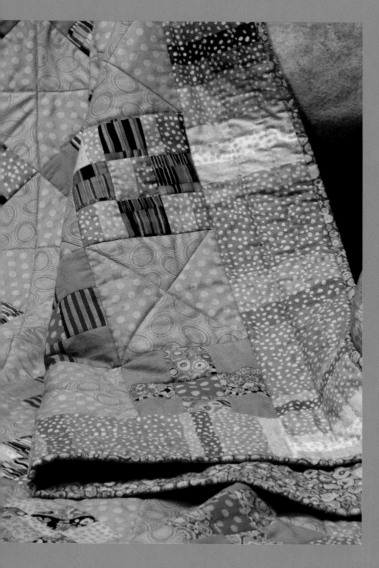

Jumping Jupiter
by Julie Stockler

The jewel tones of Julie Stockler's *Jumping Jupiter* quilt sing out in this richly furnished Moroccan room. A woman in the market shows the native love of pattern and a furniture-painting workshop in Fez demonstrates the talent for colour that lit up our visit to this magic land.

49

Cayenne
by Corienne Kramer

The forest depth of green in the private hamam in one of the stunning rooms at Café Fez shows off the fiery reds of the *Cayenne* quilt by Corienne Kramer. To add depth to her reds, she backed it with red Millefiore.

flying geese **

Kaffe Fassett

The centre of this quilt is made using triangles (Template H) which are pieced into rows. The row ends are completed using a second triangle (Template J), which is also used in the border corner posts to create the illusion of a mitred corner to the simple border.

SIZE OF QUILT
The finished quilt will measure approx. 63in x 77in (160cm x 195.5cm).

MATERIALS
Patchwork Fabrics
SHIRT STRIPES

Brown	GP51BR	⅜yd (35cm)
Cobalt	GP51CB	¼yd (25cm)
SPOT		
Duck Egg	GP70DE	¾yd (70cm)
ABORIGINAL DOTS		
Silver	GP71SV	⅜yd (35cm)
Taupe	GP71TA	⅞yd (80cm)
OMBRE		
Purple	GP117PU	½yd (45cm)
PEKING		
Orange	GP130OR	⅜yd (35cm)
FLAME STRIPE		
Red	GP134RD	½yd (45cm)
SURREY		
Black	GP135BK	¾yd (70cm)
Cobalt	GP135CB	⅜yd (35cm)
Grey	GP135GY	½yd (45cm)
JOY		
Blue	PJ60BL	½yd (45cm)
Brown	PJ60BR	½yd (45cm)
SHOT COTTON		
Sky	SC62	⅜yd (35cm)
Aqua	SC77	⅝yd (60cm)
WOVEN CATERPILLAR STRIPE		
Blue	WCS BL	¼yd (25cm)

Border Fabric
ZIGZAG

Cool	BM43CL	1yd (90cm)

Backing Fabric 5yd (4.6m)
We suggest these fabrics for backing
CAMELLIA Brown, GP132BR
JOY Brown, PJ60BR

Binding
SPOT

Black	GP70BK	⅝yd (60cm)

Batting
71in x 85in (180.5cm x 216cm)

Quilting thread
Toning machine quilting thread

Templates

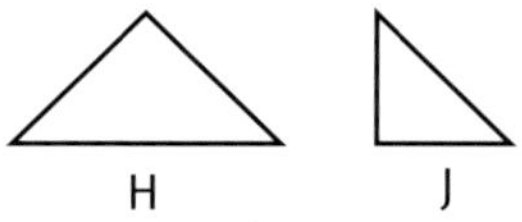

H   J

CUTTING OUT
Template H Cut 4 ⅛in (10.5cm) strips across the width of the fabric. Each strip will give you 8 triangles per full width. Place the template with the long side along the cut edge of the strip, this will ensure the long side of the triangles will not have a bias edge. Cut 50 in GP71TA, 34 in GP70DE, 26 in SC77, 23 in GP117PU, 22 in GP135GY, 21 in PJ60BR, 19 in GP134RD, 18 in PJ60BL, 15 in GP130OR, 14 in SC62, 13 in GP71SV, 12 in GP51BR, 11 in GP135BK, 9 in GP135CB, 8 in GP51CB and 5 in WCS BL. Total 300 triangles.

Template J Cut 4⅜in (11cm) strips across the width of the fabric. Each strip will give you 18 triangles per full width. Cut 40 in GP135BK. In fabric BM34CL cut 4 squares 4⅜in x 4⅜in (11cm x 11cm), align the zigzag stripes in the fabric design vertically then cut 2 squares diagonally from top left to bottom right, then cut the other 2 squares diagonally from top right to bottom left. This will enable you to piece 4 half square triangle corner posts for the border with the stripe directions matching the borders to create the illusion of mitred corners.

Borders Cut 7 strips 4in (10.25cm) wide across the width of the fabric. Join as necessary and cut 2 borders 70½in x 4in (179cm x 10.25cm) for the quilt sides and 2 borders 56½in x 4in (143.5cm x 10.25cm) for the quilt top and bottom in BM43CL.

Binding Cut 8 strips 2½in (6.5cm) wide across the width of the fabric in GP70BK.

Backing Cut 1 piece 40in x 85in (101.5cm x 216cm) and 1 piece 32in x 85in (81.25cm x 216cm) backing fabric.

MAKING THE QUILT
Use a ¼in (6mm) seam allowance throughout. Refer to the quilt assembly diagram for fabric placement. Piece a total of 20 rows as shown in the quilt assembly diagram. Join the rows to complete the quilt centre.

ADDING THE BORDERS
To make the border corner posts take 2 triangles and align the stripe direction so that they will produce the illusion of a mitred corner, stitch into a half square triangle block, make 4. Add the side borders to the quilt centre, then add a pieced corner post to each end of the top and bottom borders, making sure the stripe direction is consistent. Join the top and bottom borders to the centre to complete the quilt.

FINISHING THE QUILT
Press the quilt top. Seam the backing pieces using a ¼in (6mm) seam allowance to form a piece approx. 71in x 85in (180.5cm x 216cm). Layer the quilt top, batting and backing and baste together (see page 140). Using toning machine quilting stitch in the ditch throughout the quilt. Trim the quilt edges and attach the binding (see page 141).

QUILT ASSEMBLY DIAGRAM

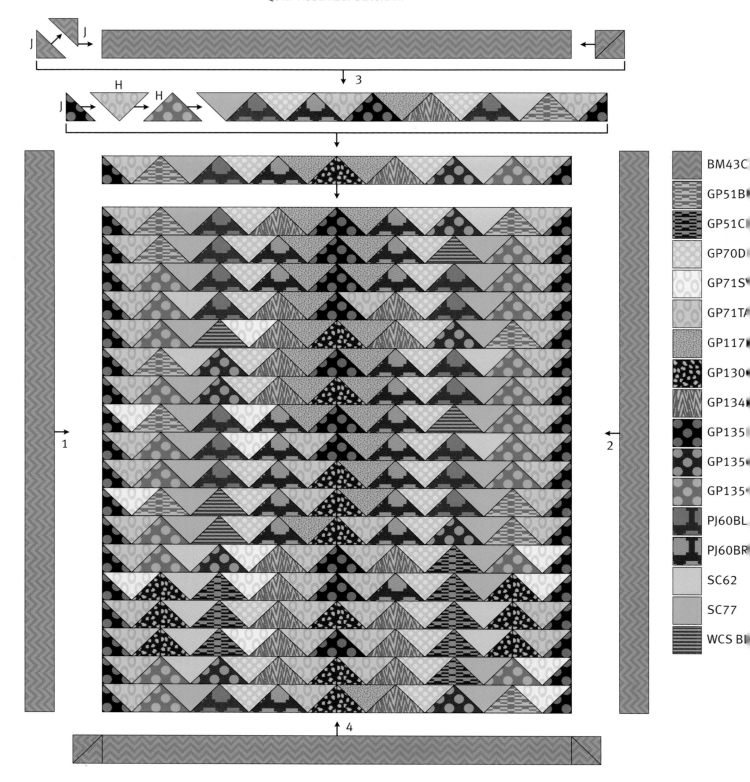

BM43C

GP51B

GP51C

GP70D

GP71S

GP71TA

GP117

GP130

GP134

GP135

GP135

GP135

PJ60BL

PJ60BR

SC62

SC77

WCS B

strata *

Kaffe Fassett

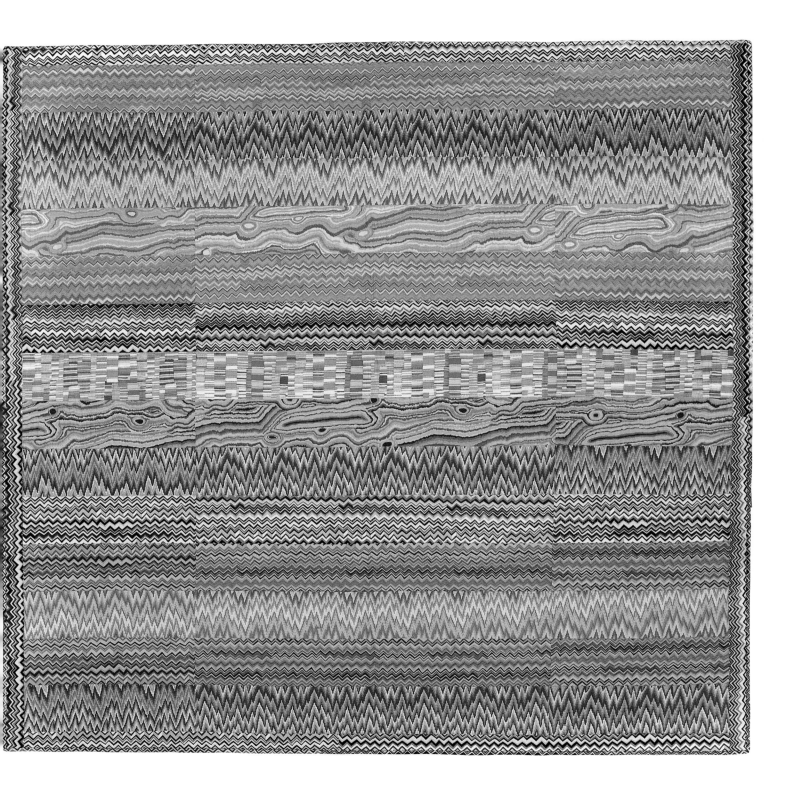

The centre of this very straightforward quilt is made using strips cut to size across the width of the fabric. The strips are sewn to form layers which resemble rock formations known as strata. The centre is surrounded with a simple border.

SIZE OF QUILT
The finished quilt will measure approx. 82½in x 81in (209.5cm x 205.75cm).

MATERIALS
Patchwork and Border Fabrics
ZIGZAG
Multi	BM43MU	¾yd (70cm)
Pink	BM43PK	¾yd (70cm)
White	BM43WH	1½yd (1.4m)

SHIRT STRIPES
Midnight Chalk	GP51MC	½yd (45cm)

JUPITER
Purple	GP131PU	½yd (45cm)
Stone	GP131ST	½yd (45cm)

FLAME STRIPE
Pastel	GP134PT	1¼yd (1.15m)
Yellow	GP134YE	¾yd (70cm)

Backing Fabric 6¼yd (5.7m)
We suggest these fabrics for backing
GUINEA FLOWER White, GP59WH
JUPITER Purple, GP131PU

Binding
ZIGZAG
White	BM43WH	¾yd (70cm)

Batting
90in x 89in (228.5cm x 226cm)

Quilting thread
Toning machine quilting thread and a selection of toning perlé embroidery threads.

CUTTING OUT
Strips Cut 6in (15.25cm) strips across the width of the fabric. Cut 6 in GP134PT, 4 in BM43MU, BM43PK, BM43WH, GP134YE, 2 in GP51MC, GP131PU and GP131ST. Total 28 strips.
Borders Cut 9 strips 2½in (6.25cm) wide across the width of the fabric in BM43WH. Join as necessary and cut 2 borders 81½in x 2½in (207cm x 6.25cm) for the quilt sides and 2 borders 79in x 2½in (200.5cm x 6.25cm) for the quilt top and bottom.

Binding Cut 9 strips 2½in (6.5cm) wide across the width of the fabric in BM43WH.

Backing Cut 2 pieces 40in x 89in (101.5cm x 226cm), 2 pieces 40in x 11in (101.5cm x 28cm) and 1 piece 11in x 10in (28cm x 25.5cm) in backing fabric.

MAKING THE QUILT
Use a ¼in (6mm) seam allowance throughout. Refer to the quilt assembly diagram for fabric placement. Each row of the quilt centre is made using 2 strips of the same fabric. From 2 strips cut 1 piece 40in x 6in (101.5cm x 15.25cm) for the centre section of the row and 2

56

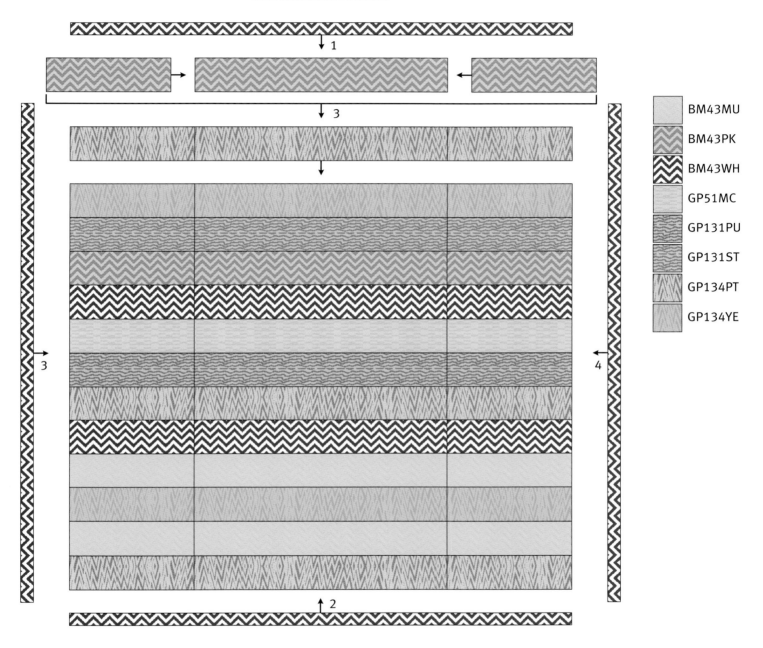

pieces 20in x 6in (50.75cm x 15.25cm) for the ends of the row. Join the 3 strips to form a row as shown in the quilt assembly diagram. Make 14 rows in total. Lay out your rows in the correct order as shown in the quilt assembly diagram. Press the seam allowances in opposite directions for each row and join the rows to complete the quilt centre.

ADDING THE BORDERS
Add the top and bottom borders to the quilt centre, then join the side borders to the centre as shown in the quilt assembly diagram to complete the quilt.

FINISHING THE QUILT
Press the quilt top. Seam the backing pieces using a ¼in (6mm) seam allowance to form a piece approx. 90in

x 89in (228.5cm x 226cm). Layer the quilt top, batting and backing and baste together (see page 140). Using toning machine quilting thread stitch in the ditch in all the seams, then hand quilt using perlé embroidery threads outlining some of the zigzags and other linear elements in the fabric designs. Trim the quilt edges and attach the binding (see page 141).

sunny snowballs **

Kaffe Fassett

The centre of this quilt is made using traditional Snowball blocks, the shapes are an octagon and four triangles, in this case it is made 'the easy way' by using a large square (Template T) and 4 small squares (Template U) for each block. The small squares are placed over the corners of the large squares and stitched diagonally. They are then trimmed and flipped back to replace the corners of the large square. The quilt is completed with a simple border with pieced corner posts, made using a triangle (cut to size) which gives the illusion of mitred corners.

SIZE OF QUILT
The finished quilt will measure approx. 56in x 66in (142.25cm x 167.5cm).

MATERIALS
Patchwork Fabrics
CRACKLE
Grey   BM39GY   ¼yd (25cm)
JOLLY
Yellow   BM40YE   ¼yd (25cm)
POMEGRANATE
Yellow   BM41YE   ¼yd (25cm)
ZIGZAG
Multi   BM43MU   ¼yd (25cm)
GUINEA FLOWER
Apricot   GP59AP   ¼yd (25cm)
Yellow   GP59YE   ¼yd (25cm)
SPOT
Gold   GP70GD   ¼yd (25cm)
ABORIGINAL DOTS
Lilac   GP71LI   ⅞yd (80cm)
PEKING
Rust   GP130RU   ¼yd (25cm)
JUPITER
Purple   GP131PU   ¼yd (25cm)
CAMELLIA
Pastel   GP132PT   ¼yd (25cm)
FLAME STRIPE
Pastel   GP134PT   ¼yd (25cm)
Yellow   GP134YE   ¼yd (25cm)
SURREY
Turquoise   GP135TQ   ¼yd (25cm)
UZBEKISTAN
Yellow   GP136YE   ¼yd (25cm)
JOY
Yellow   PJ60YE   ¼yd (25cm)

Border Fabric
RIBBON STRIPE
Yellow   GP137YE   1⅝yd (1.5m)

Backing Fabric 3⅞yd (3.5m)
We suggest these fabrics for backing
CHARD Spring, GP128SP
CAMELLIA Pastel, GP132PT

Binding
GUINEA FLOWER
Turquoise   GP59TQ   ⅝yd (60cm)

Batting
64in x 74in (162.5cm x 188cm)

Quilting thread
Toning machine quilting thread.

Templates

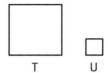

T   U

CUTTING OUT
Borders Cut 5 strips 8½in (21.5cm) wide across the width of the fabric. Join as necessary and cut 2 borders 50½in x 8½in (128.25cm x 21.5in) for the quilt sides and 2 borders 40½in x 8½in (102.75cm x 21.5cm) for the quilt top and bottom in GP137YE.
Border Corner Posts Cut an 8⅞in (22.5cm) strip across the width of the fabric in GP137YE, cut 4 squares 8⅞in x 8⅞in (22.5cm x 22.5cm), align the stripes in the fabric design vertically then cut 2 squares diagonally from top left to bottom right, then cut the other 2 squares diagonally from top right to bottom left. This will enable you to piece 4 half square triangle corner posts with the stripe directions matching the borders to create the illusion of mitred corners.
Template T Cut 5½in (14cm) strips across the width of the fabric. Each strip

will give you 7 squares per full width. Cut 6 in BM41YE, BM43MU, GP59AP, GP70GD, GP132PT, GP134PT, GP134YE, GP135TQ, PJ60YE, 5 in BM39GY, BM40YE, GP59YE, GP136YE, 4 in GP131PU and 2 in GP130RU. Total 80 squares.
Template U Cut 1¾in (4.5cm) strips across the width of the fabric. Each strip will give you 22 squares per full width. Cut 320 in GP71LI.

Binding Cut 7 strips 2½in (6.5cm) wide across the width of the fabric in GP59TQ.

Backing Cut 1 piece 40in x 64in (101.5cm x 162.5cm) and 1 piece 35in x 64in (89cm x 162.5cm) in backing fabric.

MAKING THE BLOCKS
Use a ¼in (6mm) seam allowance throughout. Refer to the quilt assembly diagram for fabric placement. To make the Snowball blocks take one large square (template T) and four small squares (template U). Place one small square, right sides together onto each corner of the large square, matching the edges carefully as shown in block assembly diagram a. Stitch diagonally across the small squares as shown in diagram b. Trim the corners to a ¼in (6mm) seam allowance and press the corners out (diagram c). Make 80 snowball blocks.

Finally make 4 border corner posts, take 2 triangles and align the stripe direction so that they will produce the illusion of a mitred corner, stitch into a half square triangle block, make 4 and reserve until you are ready to add the border to the quilt centre.

MAKING THE QUILT
Join the blocks into 10 rows of 8 blocks. Join the rows to complete the quilt

BLOCK ASSEMBLY DIAGRAMS

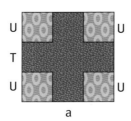
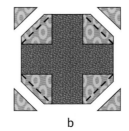
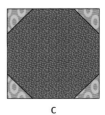

a   b   c

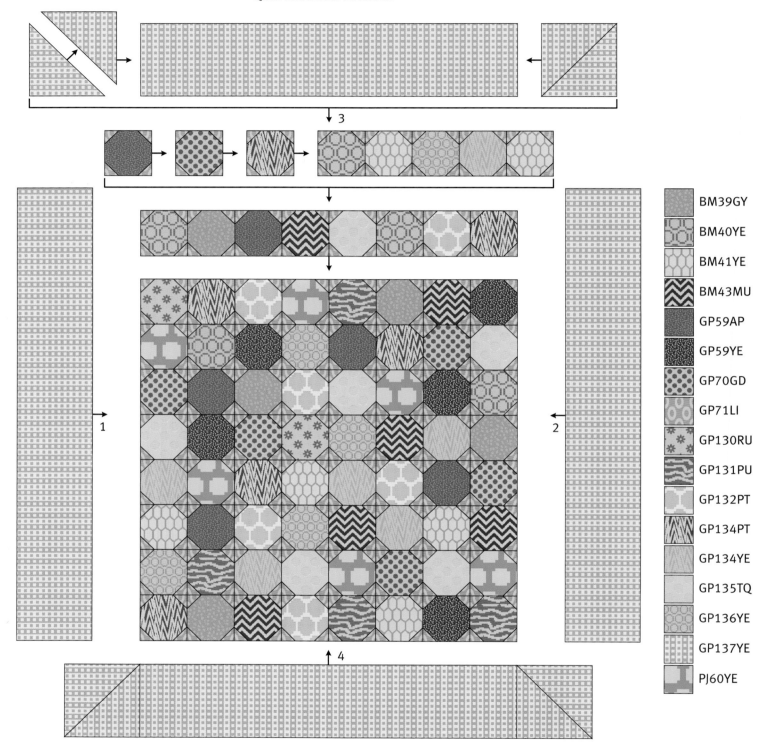

	BM39GY
	BM40YE
	BM41YE
	BM43MU
	GP59AP
	GP59YE
	GP70GD
	GP71LI
	GP130RU
	GP131PU
	GP132PT
	GP134PT
	GP134YE
	GP135TQ
	GP136YE
	GP137YE
	PJ60YE

centre. Add the side borders to the quilt centre, then add a pieced border corner post to each end of the top and bottom borders, making sure the stripe direction is consistent. Join the top and bottom borders to the centre to complete the quilt.

FINISHING THE QUILT
Press the quilt top. Seam the backing pieces using a ¼in (6mm) seam allowance to form a piece approx. 64in x 74in (162.5cm x 188cm). Layer the quilt top, batting and backing and baste together

(see page 140). Using toning machine quilting thread stitch in the ditch throughout the quilt. Trim the quilt edges and attach the binding (see page 141).

60

paisley columns **

Kaffe Fassett

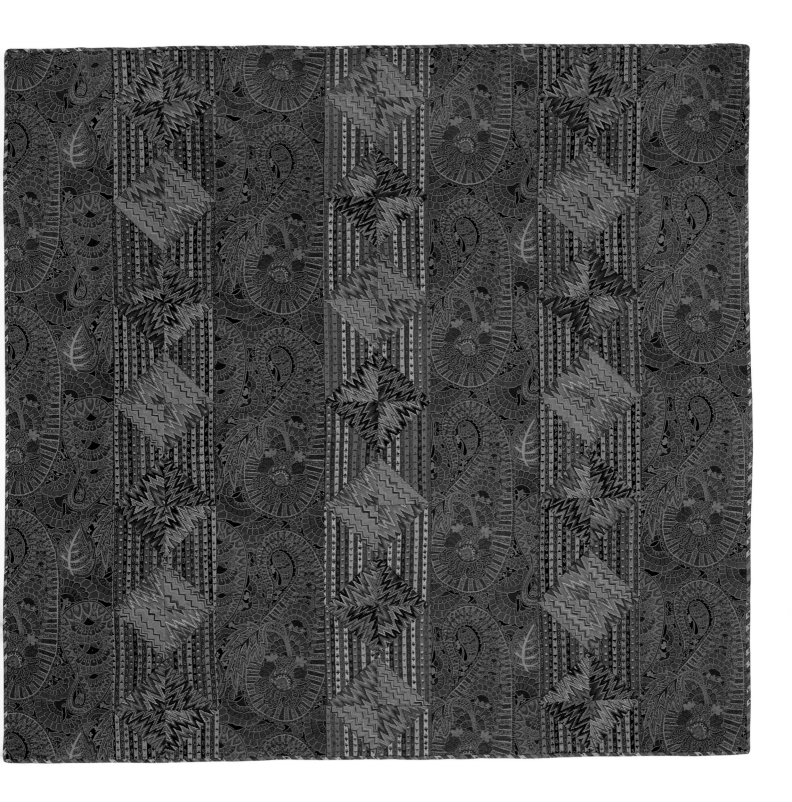

Hourglass blocks made using a triangle (Template QQ) are set on point in columns using a second triangle (Template RR). You'll find half template RR on page 135. Take a large piece of paper, fold, place the edge of template RR to the fold of paper, trace around shape and cut out. Open out for the complete template. Template QQ is used again to fill the column ends. The pieced columns are alternated with large sections of Kaffe's striking Belle Epoch paisley design fabric, hence the quilt name.

SIZE OF QUILT
The finished quilt will measure approx. 82½in x 80½in (209.5cm x 204.5cm).

MATERIALS
Patchwork Fabrics
ZIGZAG
Cool	BM43CL	½yd (45cm)

BELLE EPOCH
Dark	GP133DK	4¾yd (4.4m)

FLAME STRIPE
Brown	GP134BR	⅝yd (60cm)
Dark	GP134DK	⅝yd (60cm)
Red	GP134RD	½yd (45cm)

RIBBON STRIPE
Blue	GP137BL	⅞yd (80cm)
Smoky	GP137SM	1¼yd (1.15m)

Backing Fabric 6⅛yd (5.6m)
We suggest these fabrics for backing
MILLEFIORE Red, GP92RD
UZBEKISTAN Brown, GP136BR

Binding
RIBBON STRIPE
Blue	GP137BL	¾yd (70cm)

Batting
90in x 88in (228.5cm x 223.5cm)

Quilting thread
Toning machine and/or hand quilting thread.

Templates

 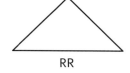

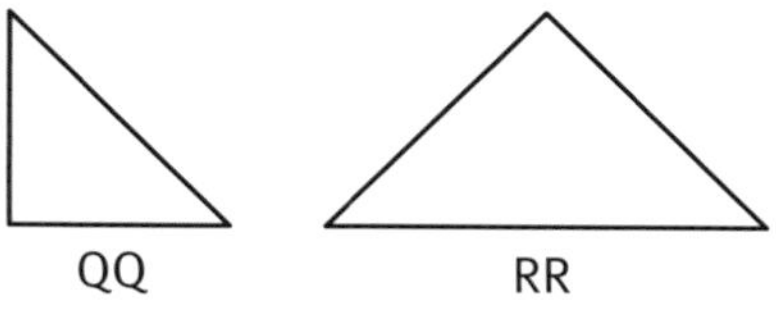

QQ   RR

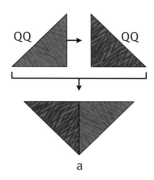 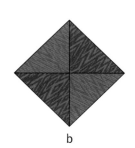

QQ   QQ

a   b

CUTTING OUT
Cut the fabric in the order stated to prevent waste. Please note that template QQ is cut in 2 ways depending on where it will be used in the quilt. For Template RR the Ribbon Stripe fabric is cut so that the stripes will run vertically down the columns. Please read the whole instruction carefully before starting.
Template QQ For Hourglass Blocks. Cut 4¾in (12cm) strips across the width of the fabric, each strip will give you 7 triangles per full width. Place the long side of the triangle template along the cut edge of the fabric, this will ensure the edges of the blocks will not have a bias edge and the zigzags in the fabric designs will run correctly. Cut 22 in GP134BR, GP134DK, 20 in BM43CL and GP134RD. Total 84 triangles.
Template QQ For Setting Triangles. Cut 6⅝in (16.75cm) squares, cut each square diagonally to form 2 triangles. Cut 8 in GP137SM and 4 in GP137BL. Total 12 triangles
Template RR Cut 6⅜in (16.25cm) strips down the length of the fabric. Cut triangles using the template so that the stripes run along the long side. Cut 24 in GP137SM and 12 in GP137BL. Total 36 triangles.
BELLE EPOCH Columns Cut 4 columns down the length of the fabric 12½in x 81in (31.75cm x 205.75cm) in GP133DK.

Binding Cut 9⅜yd (8.6m) of 2½in (6.5cm) wide bias binding in GP137BL.

Backing Cut 2 pieces 40in x 90in (101.5cm x 228.5cm), 2 pieces 40in x 9in (101.5cm x 22.75cm) and 1 piece 11in x 9in (28cm x 22.75cm) in backing fabric.

MAKING THE BLOCKS
Use a ¼in (6mm) seam allowance throughout. Refer to the quilt assembly diagram for fabric placement. Handle the pieces for the blocks carefully as there are lots of bias edges, take extra care not to distort the pieces as they are fed through the sewing machine. Piece a total of 21 hourglass blocks as shown in block assembly diagram a, the finished block can be seen in diagram b.

MAKING THE QUILT
Lay out the blocks in 3 columns as shown in the quilt assembly diagram. Fill in the column sides with the template RR triangles and the column corners with the template QQ setting triangles. Piece the columns as shown in the quilt assembly diagram. Join the pieced columns to the GP134DK columns to complete the quilt.

FINISHING THE QUILT
Press the quilt top. Seam the backing pieces using a ¼in (6mm) seam allowance to form a piece approx. 90in x 88in (228.5cm x 223.5cm). Layer the quilt top, batting and backing and baste together (see page 140). Using toning machine quilting thread quilt in the ditch throughout the quilt, then by hand or machine quilt the GP133DK columns following the large paisley designs in the fabric. Trim the quilt edges and attach the binding (see page 141).

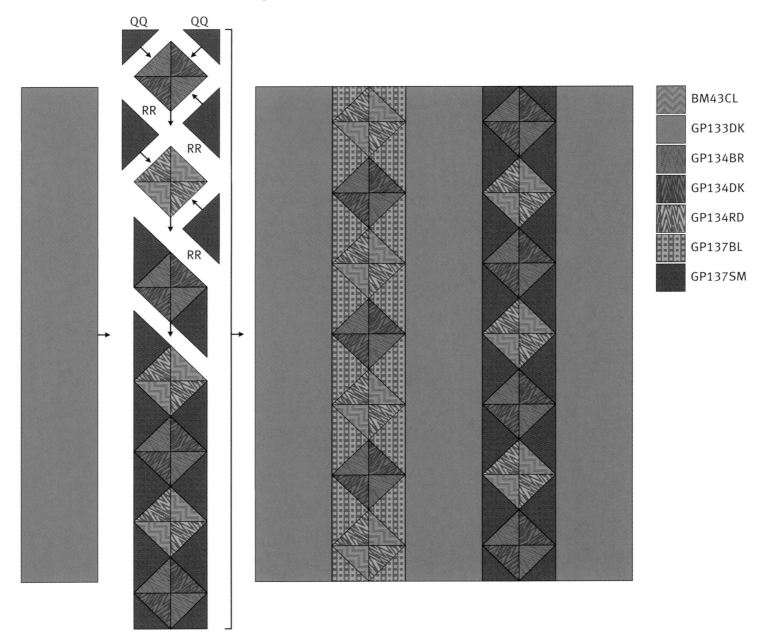

QQ QQ

RR

RR

RR

BM43CL
GP133DK
GP134BR
GP134DK
GP134RD
GP137BL
GP137SM

shuttles **

Kaffe Fassett

The blocks that make up the centre of this quilt are an elongated hexagon along with 4 triangles. The blocks are pieced using a rectangle (Template V) and 4 squares (Template W). The squares are placed over the corners of the rectangle and stitched diagonally. They are then trimmed and flipped back to replace the corners of the rectangle. The quilt is completed with a twisted ribbon border, pieced using 2 lozenge shapes (Template X & Reverse X and Y) together with a triangle (Template Z).

SIZE OF QUILT
The finished quilt will measure approx. 49in x 63in (124.5cm x 160cm).

MATERIALS
Patchwork and Border Fabrics
MAD PLAID
Pastel   BM37PT   ³⁄₈yd (35cm)
CRACKLE
Red   BM39RD   ¼yd (25cm)
ROMAN GLASS
Blue and White   GP01BW   ³⁄₈yd (35cm)
SPOT
Periwinkle   GP70PE   ¼yd (25cm)
ABORIGINAL DOTS
Iris   GP71IR   ³⁄₄yd (70cm)
Pear   GP71PR   ½yd (45cm)
Terracotta   GP71TC   ¼yd (25cm)
OMBRE
Moss   GP117MS   ³⁄₈yd (35cm)
ORIENTAL TREES
Stone   GP129ST   ³⁄₈yd (35cm)
RIBBON STRIPE
Yellow   GP137YE   ¼yd (25cm)
SHOT COTTON
Tangerine   SC11   ³⁄₈yd (35cm)
Lavender   SC14   ⁵⁄₈yd (60cm)
Ecru   SC24   ¼yd (25cm)
Apple   SC39   ³⁄₈yd (35cm)
Jade   SC41   ³⁄₈yd (35cm)
Sky   SC62   ³⁄₈yd (35cm)
Pudding   SC68   ³⁄₈yd (35cm)
Aqua   SC77   ¼yd (25cm)
Apricot   SC79   ¼yd (25cm)
Shell   SC100SH   ³⁄₈yd (35cm)

Backing Fabric 3³⁄₈yd (3.1m)
We suggest these fabrics for backing
MILLEFIORE Green, GP92GN
SPOT Periwinkle, GP70PE

Binding
ABORIGINAL DOTS
Iris   GP71IR   ½yd (45cm)

Batting
57in x 71in (144.75cm x 180.25cm)

Quilting thread
Toning machine quilting thread.

Templates

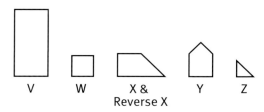

V   W   X & Reverse X   Y   Z

CUTTING OUT
Template V Cut 4in (10.25cm) strips across the width of the fabric. Each strip will give you 5 rectangles per full width. Cut 6 in GP117MS, SC41, 5 in BM39RD, GP70PE, GP71IR, GP71TC, GP129ST, GP137YE, SC11, SC14, SC39, SC62, SC68, SC79, 4 in BM37PT, GP01BW, GP71PR, SC24, SC77 and SC100SH. Total 96 rectangles.

Template W Cut 2¼in (5.75cm) strips across the width of the fabric. Each strip will give you 17 squares per full width. Cut 28 in BM37PT, SC14, SC39, 24 in GP01BW, GP71IR, 20 in GP71PR, GP129ST, SC11, SC62, SC100SH, 16 in BM39RD, GP70PE, GP71TC, GP117MS, GP137YE, SC41, SC77, SC79, 12 in SC24 and SC68. Total 384 squares.

Template X and Reverse X Cut 3in (7.5cm) strips across the width of the fabric. Each strip will give you 8 patches per full width. Cut 14 in GP71IR and SC14. Reverse the template by turning it over and cut 16 in GP71IR and 12 in SC14. Total 56 patches. Reserve leftover fabric for template Y.

Template Y Cut 4 in SC14.

Template Z Cut 2⁵⁄₈in (6.5cm) strips across the width of the fabric. Each strip will give you 30 triangles per full width. Cut 60 in GP71PR, SC68 and 4 in SC14. Total 124 triangles.

Binding Cut 6 strips 2½in (6.5cm) wide across the width of the fabric in GP71IR.

Backing Cut 1 piece 40in x 57in (101.5cm x 144.75cm) and 1 piece 32in x 57in (81.25cm x 144.75cm) in backing fabric.

MAKING THE BLOCKS
Use a ¼in (6mm) seam allowance throughout. Refer to the quilt assembly diagram for fabric placement. To make a block take one rectangle (template V) and four squares of the same fabric (template W). Place 2 squares, right sides together onto 2 opposite corners of the rectangle, matching the edges carefully as shown in block assembly diagram a. Stitch diagonally across the squares and trim the corners to a ¼in (6mm) seam allowance as shown in diagram b. Press the corners out (diagram c). Next place the remaining 2 squares onto the other 2 corners of the rectangle, again matching the edges carefully as shown in block assembly diagram d. Stitch diagonally across the squares and trim the corners to a ¼in (6mm) seam allowance as before (diagram e). Finally press the corners out to complete the block as shown in diagram f. Make 96 blocks.

MAKING THE BORDERS
Lay out the border pieces as shown in the quilt assembly diagram. Sub-piece units of 1 template X or Reverse X patch with 2 template Z triangles as shown in border unit assembly diagram g and h. The complete unit is shown in diagram i. Complete the border ends with the template Y patches as shown in the quilt assembly diagram

MAKING THE QUILT
Join the blocks into 8 rows of 12 blocks. Join the rows to complete the quilt centre. Join the side borders to the quilt centre, followed by the top and bottom borders as shown in the quilt assembly diagram to complete the quilt.

FINISHING THE QUILT
Press the quilt top. Seam the backing pieces using a ¼in (6mm) seam allowance to form a piece approx. 57in x 71in (144.75cm x 180.25cm). Layer the quilt top, batting and backing and baste together (see page 140). Using toning machine quilting thread quilt as shown in the quilting diagram. Trim the quilt edges and attach the binding (see page 141).

BLOCK ASSEMBLY DIAGRAMS

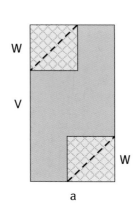

a

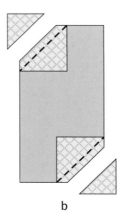

b

c

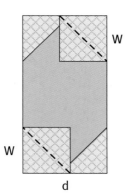

d

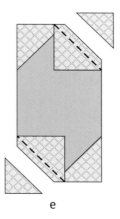

e

f

BORDER UNIT ASSEMBLY DIAGRAMS

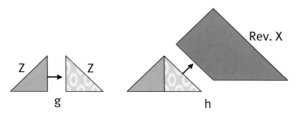

g

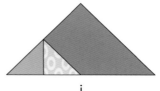

Rev. X

h

i

QUILTING DIAGRAM

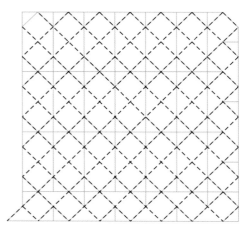

66

QUILT ASSEMBLY DIAGRAM

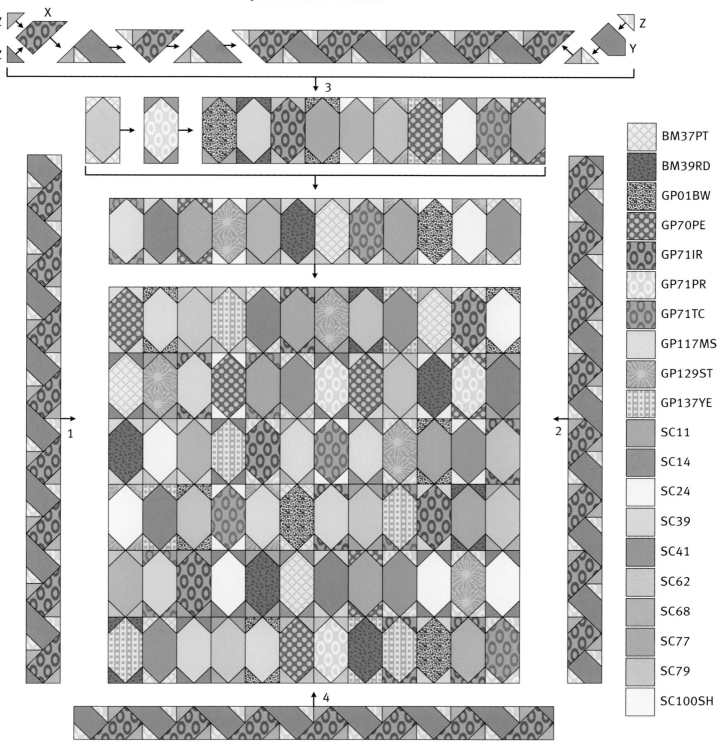

BM37PT

BM39RD

GP01BW

GP70PE

GP71IR

GP71PR

GP71TC

GP117MS

GP129ST

GP137YE

SC11

SC14

SC24

SC39

SC41

SC62

SC68

SC77

SC79

SC100SH

library **

Kaffe Fassett

All the shapes for this quilt are cut to size and no templates are provided. The blocks are made by cutting a series of varied length strips to represent books. These are pieced with a background fabric, trimmed equally and joined to form rectangular blocks. The blocks are then interspaced and surrounded with sashing and a pieced border. We have drawn Kaffe's quilt as accurately as possible, but this meant to be an adventure, so we have not stated exact numbers and sizes of 'books' to cut. Your quilt can include any fabrics and book sizes you like!

SIZE OF QUILT
The finished quilt will measure approx. 65in x 85½in (165cm x 217.25cm).

MATERIALS
Book Patchwork Fabrics
ABORIGINAL DOTS

Iris	GP71IR	¼yd (25cm)

OMBRE

Blue	GP117BL	⅜yd (35cm)
Green	GP117GN	¼yd (25cm)
Red	GP117RD	⅜yd (35cm)

SHOT COTTON

Ginger	SC01	¼yd (25cm)
Persimmon	SC07	¼yd (25cm)
Raspberry	SC08	¼yd (25cm)
Chartreuse	SC12	¼yd (25cm)
Smoky	SC20	¼yd (25cm)
Jade	SC41	⅜yd (35cm)
Nut	SC53	¼yd (25cm)
Sky	SC62	¼yd (25cm)
Bronze	SC69	¼yd (25cm)
Clementine	SC80	¼yd (25cm)
Magenta	SC81	¼yd (25cm)
Lipstick	SC82	¼yd (25cm)
Curry	SC84	¼yd (25cm)
Blueberry	SC88	¼yd (25cm)
Pea Soup	SC91	⅜yd (35cm)
Cactus	SC92	⅜yd (35cm)

Sashing, Border and Binding Fabrics
SHOT COTTON

Sandstone	SC86	1⅞yd (1.7m)
Blue Jeans	SC100BJ	2¼yd (2.1m)

Backing Fabric 5½yd (5m)
We suggest these fabrics for backing
OMBRE Red, GP117RD or Blue, GP117BL

Batting
73in x 93in (185.5cm x 236.25cm)

Quilting thread
Toning perlé embroidery threads.

CUTTING OUT
Cut the fabric in the order stated to prevent waste.

Inner Border Cut 8 strips 3in (7.5cm) wide across the width of the fabric in SC100BJ. Join as necessary and cut 2 borders 79in x 3in (200.5cm x 7.5cm) for the quilt sides and 2 borders 65½in x 3in (166.25cm x 7.5cm) for the quilt top and bottom.

Outer Border Cut 8 strips 1½in (3.75cm) wide across the width of the fabric in SC86. Join as necessary and cut 2 borders 79in x 1½in (200.5cm x 3.75cm) for the quilt sides and 2 borders 65½in x 1½in (166.25cm x 3.75cm) for the quilt top and bottom.

Vertical Sashing Cut 1½in (3.75cm) strips across the width of the fabric, each strip will give you 2 sashing strips per full width. Cut 20 sashing strips 15in x 1½in (38cm x 3.75cm) in SC86.

Horizontal Sashing Cut 9 strips 1½in (3.75cm) wide across the width of the fabric in SC86. Join as necessary and cut 6 sashing strips 58½in x 1½in (148.5cm x 3.75cm).

Books These strips are cut at 2in (5cm) wide and vary in length from 8½in to 12½in (21.5cm to 31.75cm). You will need a total of 180 book strips.

Background Cut 2in (5cm) wide strips across the width of the fabric. The number needed will vary depending on the length of the books you cut, so cut a few at a time. You will probably end up using about 23 strips.

Binding Cut 8 strips 2½in (6.5cm) wide across the width of the fabric in SC86.

Backing Cut 1 piece 40in x 93in (101.5cm x 236.25cm) and 1 piece 34in x 93in (86.25cm x 236.25cm) in backing fabric.

MAKING THE BLOCKS

Use a ¼in (6mm) seam allowance throughout. Refer to the quilt assembly diagram for fabric placement. For your first block cut 12 book strips, vary the lengths as you please. Take a background strip and place the first book strip right sides together and stitch along one short side. See block assembly diagram a. Open out the fabrics and trim the background strip so that the pieced section measures 15in (38cm) long as shown in diagram b. Do the same with the remaining 11 book strips. Join the pieced strips as shown in diagram c. The finished block is shown in diagram d. Make 15 blocks.

MAKING THE QUILT

Lay out the blocks in 5 rows of 3 blocks, interspace with the vertical and horizontal sashing strips, as shown in the quilt assembly diagram. Separate into rows and join. Join the rows to complete the quilt centre. The borders are added in an unusual order which gives the clever bookcase effect, refer to the photograph and quilt assembly diagram for help with this. Stitch the side inner borders to the side outer borders, then add to the quilt sides. Stitch the top and bottom inner borders to the top and bottom outer borders, then join them to the quilt centre to complete the quilt.

FINISHING THE QUILT

Press the quilt top. Seam the backing pieces using a ¼in (6mm) seam allowance to form a piece approx. 73in x 93in (185.5cm x 236.25cm). Layer the quilt top, batting and backing and baste together (see page 140). Using toning perlé embroidery threads quilt as shown in the quilting diagram. Vary the position of the quilting lines in the background SC100BJ sections for each block, refer to the photograph for help with this. Trim the quilt edges and attach the binding (see page 141)

BLOCK ASSEMBLY DIAGRAMS

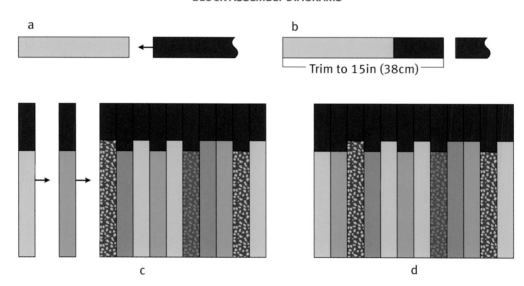

a

b

Trim to 15in (38cm)

c

d

QUILTING DIAGRAM

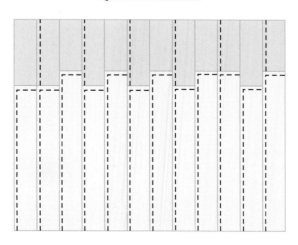

Kaffe says:
You can speed up the piecing process by having several background strips on the go at a time, chain piece a few book strips to background strips, then press and trim them all at the same time.

QUILT ASSEMBLY DIAGRAM

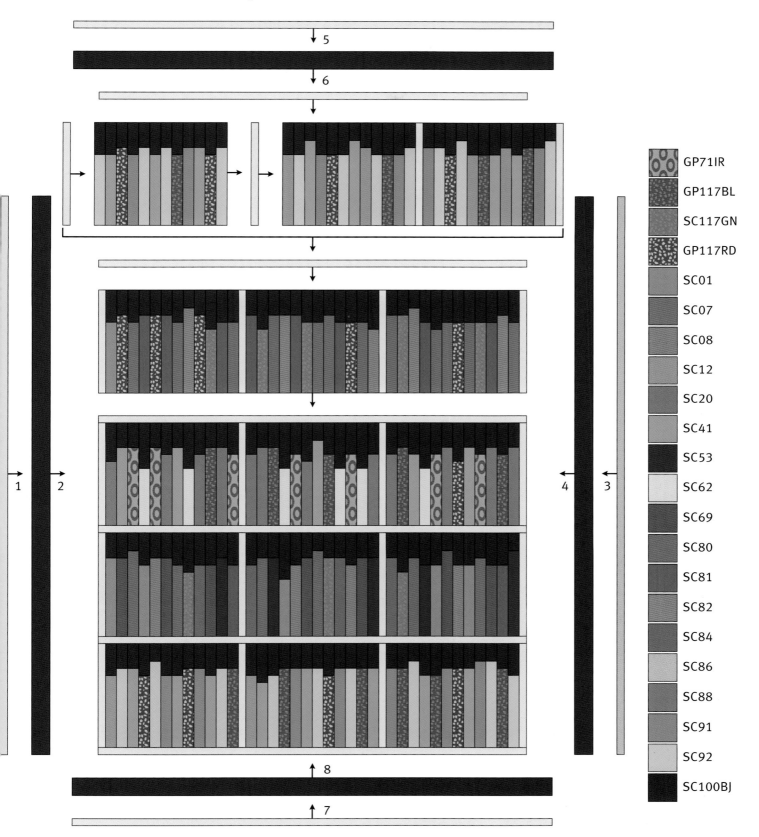

GP71IR

GP117BL

SC117GN

GP117RD

SC01

SC07

SC08

SC12

SC20

SC41

SC53

SC62

SC69

SC80

SC81

SC82

SC84

SC86

SC88

SC91

SC92

SC100BJ

water garden **

Kaffe Fassett

Traditional 'square in a square' blocks which finish to 12in (30.5cm) square are pieced using a square (Large Square), cut to size and a triangle (Template G). The blocks are straight set in rows, interspaced and surrounded by pieced sashing and corner posts made using 4 rectangles (Sashing Wide, Sashing Narrow, Corner Post Wide and Corner Post Narrow) which are all cut to size. The sashing and corner posts are pieced from Shot Cotton and Kaffe's graduated Ombre fabric and the corner posts are cleverly alternated vertically and horizontally so that combined with some fussy cutting and piecing the sashing looks like shaded woven ribbons.

SIZE OF QUILT
The finished quilt will measure approx. 84in x 84in (213.25cm x 213.25cm).

MATERIALS
Patchwork Fabrics
SPOT

Green	GP70GN	¼yd (25cm)
Periwinkle	GP70PE	½yd (45cm)
Sapphire	GP70SP	¼yd (25cm)
Pond	GP70PO	½yd (45cm)
Teal	GP70TE	½yd (45cm)
Turquoise	GP70TQ	½yd (45cm)

ABORIGINAL DOTS

Delft	GP71DF	¼yd (25cm)
Iris	GP71IR	½yd (45cm)

BIG BLOOMS

Emerald	GP91EM	⅝yd (60cm)

PEKING

Lavender	GP130LV	½yd (45cm)

BROCADE PEONY

Blue	PJ62BL	⅝yd (60cm)

LAVINIA

Blue	PJ64BL	⅜yd (35cm)
Green	PJ64GN	⅝yd (60cm)

GERTRUDE

Green	PJ65GN	⅝yd (60cm)

Sashing and Corner Post Fabrics
OMBRE

Blue	GP117BL	2yd (1.8m)

SHOT COTTON

Cactus	SC92	2¼yd (2.1m)

Backing Fabric 6⅞yd (6.3m)
We suggest these fabrics for backing
ORIENTAL TREES Blue, GP129BL
BIG BLOOMS Emerald, GP91EM

Binding
SPOT

Sapphire	GP70SP	¾yd (70cm)

Batting
92in x 92in (233.75cm x 233.75cm)

Quilting thread
Toning machine and hand quilting threads

Templates

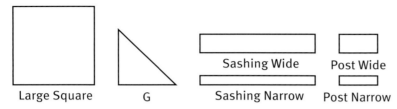

Large Square   G   Sashing Wide   Post Wide

Sashing Narrow   Post Narrow

CUTTING OUT

Cut the Corner Post Wide rectangles last, after the blocks and sashing is pieced. This allows for fussy cutting to suit the graduated fabrics. Extra fabric has been allowed for this.

Large Square Cut 9in (22.75cm) strips across the width of the fabric. Each strip will give you 4 squares per full width. Cut 6 in GP65GN, 5 in GP91GN, PJ62BL, PJ64GN and 4 in PJ64BL. Total 25 squares.

Template G Cut 6⅞in (17.5cm) strips across the width of the fabric. Each strip will give you 10 triangles per full width. Cut 16 in GP70PO, 12 in GP70PE, GP70TE, GP70TQ, GP71IR, GP130LV, 8 in GP70GN, GP70SP and GP71DF. Total 100 triangles.

Sashing Wide Cut 2½in (6.25cm) strips across the width of the fabric in GP117BL. Each strip will give you 3 rectangles per full width. Cut 12½in x 2½in (31.75cm x 6.25cm) rectangles. As far as possible the strips are organised into 2 groups of deep blue/purple and

green/pink, this adds to the shaded ribbon effect, check the photograph for help with this. Cut a total of 60 rectangles.

Sashing Narrow Cut 1½in (3.75cm) strips across the width of the fabric in SC92. Each strip will give you 3 rectangles per full width. Cut 12½in x 1½in (31.75cm x 3.75cm) rectangles. Cut a total of 120 rectangles.

Corner Post Narrow Cut 1½in (3.75cm) strips across the width of the fabric in SC92. Each strip will give you 8 rectangles per full width. Cut 4½in x 1½in (11.5cm x 3.75cm) rectangles. Cut a total of 72 rectangles.

Corner Post Wide Cut 2½in (6.25cm) strips across the width of the fabric in GP117BL. Fussy cut a total of 36 rectangles 4½in x 2½in (11.5cm x 6.25cm) to suit the fabric graduations, more detail in the instructions section.

Binding Cut 9 strips 2½in (6.25cm) wide across the width of the fabric in GP70SP.

Backing Cut 2 pieces 40in x 92in (101.5cm x 233.75cm), 2 pieces 40in x 13in (101.5cm x 33cm) and 1 piece 13in x 13in (33cm x 33cm) in backing fabric.

MAKING THE BLOCKS AND SASHING

Use a ¼in (6mm) seam allowance throughout. Refer to the quilt assembly diagram for fabric placement. Piece a total of 25 square in a square blocks as shown in block assembly diagram a, the finished block is shown in diagram b. Next piece 60 sashing strips as shown in sashing assembly diagram c, the finished strip can be seen in diagram d. Arrange the blocks and sashing on a design wall as shown in the quilt assembly diagram and the photograph. Cut Corner Post Wide rectangles to suit the colour of the sashing at the intersections in your layout, bearing in mind the orientation of the corner post. In Kaffe's quilt the top left corner needed to be dark pink and horizontal, the next post along the top row was green and vertical, the next pink and horizontal and so on throughout the quilt. Piece the fussy cut rectangles with the shot cotton to form square corner posts as shown in diagram e, the finished corner post is shown in diagram f.

MAKING THE QUILT

Add the pieced corner posts to the quilt layout as shown in the quilt assembly diagram. Piece into 11 rows, join the rows to complete the quilt.

BLOCK ASSEMBLY DIAGRAMS

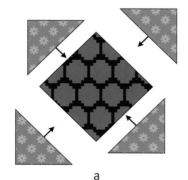

a

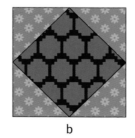

b

SASHING AND CORNER POST ASSEMBLY DIAGRAMS

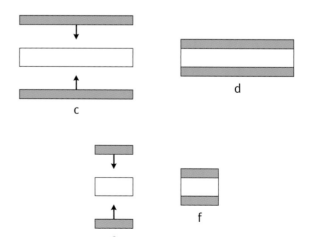

c

d

e

f

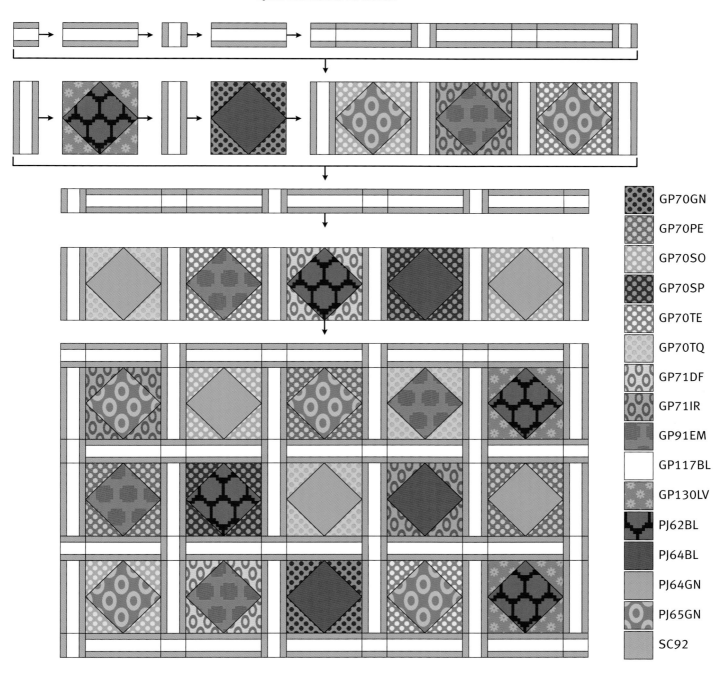

	GP70GN
	GP70PE
	GP70SO
	GP70SP
	GP70TE
	GP70TQ
	GP71DF
	GP71IR
	GP91EM
	GP117BL
	GP130LV
	PJ62BL
	PJ64BL
	PJ64GN
	PJ65GN
	SC92

FINISHING THE QUILT

Press the quilt top. Seam the backing pieces using a ¼in (6mm) seam allowance to form a piece approx. 92in x 92in (233.75cm x 233.75cm). Layer the quilt top, batting and backing and baste together (see page 140). Using toning machine quilting thread stitch in the ditch throughout the quilt. Using toning hand quilting thread hand quilt a cross from point to point in each of the block squares. Trim the quilt edges and attach the binding (see page 141).

75

pastel blush **

Kaffe Fassett

The blocks for this quilt are made using a triangle (Template G) and a square (Template EE). The square is placed over the right angle corner of the triangle, stitched diagonally then trimmed and flipped back to replace the corner. The pieced triangles are then added to another triangle to make a quarter segment of the block. The blocks are interspaced and surrounded with sashing strips (cut to size) and sashing posts (Template K). The quilt centre is then framed with a simple border with corner posts (Template AA).

SIZE OF QUILT
The finished quilt will measure approx. 69in x 83in (175.25cm x 210.75cm).

MATERIALS
Patchwork Fabrics
ABORIGINAL DOTS

Cantaloupe	GP71CA	⅛yd (15cm)
Gold	GP71GD	⅛yd (15cm)

JUPITER

Stone	GP131ST	½yd (45cm)

BROCADE PEONY

Mauve	PJ62MV	½yd (45cm)
Natural	PJ62NL	½yd (45cm)
Yellow	PJ62YE	½yd (45cm)

LAVINIA

Red	PJ64RD	½yd (45cm)

GERTRUDE

Yellow	PJ65YE	½yd (45cm)

SHOT COTTON

Sky	SC62	⅛yd (15cm)
Butter	SC64	½yd (45cm)
Apricot	SC79	½yd (45cm)
Clementine	SC80	¼yd (25cm)
Pink	SC83	½yd (45cm)
Ice	SC85	½yd (45cm)
Artemisia	SC100AR	½yd (45cm)
Shell	SC100SH	¼yd (25cm)

Sashing and Border Fabrics
GUINEA FLOWER

Mauve	GP59MV	1⅜yd (1.3m)

SPOT

Sky	GP70SK	¼yd (25cm)

CAMELLIA

Pastel	GP132PT	¼yd (25cm)

SURREY

Turquoise	GP135TQ	1⅜yd (1.3m)

Backing Fabric 5⅜yd (4.9m)
We suggest these fabrics for backing
BROCADE PEONY Natural, PJ62NL
ASIAN CIRCLES Pink, GP89PK

Binding
SPOT

Peach	GP70PH	⅝yd (60cm)

Batting
77in x 91in (195.5cm x 231.25cm)

Quilting thread
Toning machine quilting thread.

Templates

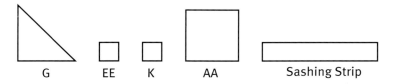

CUTTING OUT
Template G Cut 6⅞in (17.5cm) strips across the width of the fabric. Each strip will give you 10 triangles per full width. Cut 20 in SC83, 16 in PJ62MV, PJ65YE, SC85, 12 in GP131ST, PJ62NL, PJ62YE, PJ64RD, SC64, SC79, SC100AR and 8 in SC100SH. Total 160 triangles.
Template EE Cut 2in (5cm) strips across the width of the fabric. Each strip will give you 20 squares per full width. Cut 32 in SC80, 16 in GP71GD, 12 in SC62, SC83 and 8 in GP71CA. Total 80 squares.
Sashing Strips Cut 2½in (6.25cm) strips across the width of the fabric. Each strip will give you 3 sashing strips per full width. Cut 2½in x 12½in rectangles. Cut 49 in GP59MV.
Template K Cut 2½in (6.25cm) strips across the width of the fabric. Each strip will give you 16 squares per full width. Cut 30 in GP70SK.
Template AA Cut 6in (15.25cm) strips across the width of the fabric. Cut 4 in GP132PT.
Borders Cut 7 strips 6in (15.25cm) wide across the width of the fabric. Join as necessary and cut 2 borders 72½in x 6in (184.25cm x 15.25cm) for the quilt sides and 2 borders 58½in x 6in (148.5cm x 15.25cm) for the quilt top and bottom in GP135TQ.

Binding Cut 8 strips 2½in (6.5cm) wide across the width of the fabric in GP70PH.

Backing Cut 1 piece 40in x 91in (101.5cm x 231.25cm) and 1 piece 38in x 91in (96.5cm x 231.25cm) in backing fabric.

MAKING THE BLOCKS
Use a ¼in (6mm) seam allowance throughout. Refer to the quilt assembly diagram for fabric placement. To make a block take 8 template G triangles and 4 template EE squares. First replace the right angle corners of the 4 inner triangles. Place a square, right sides together onto the right angle corner of the triangle, matching the edges carefully as shown in block assembly diagram a. Stitch diagonally across the square and trim the corner to a ¼in (6mm) seam allowance as shown in diagram b. Press the corner out (diagram c). Now piece 4 segments into squares as shown in diagram d. Join 4 segments as shown in diagram e to complete a block. The completed block is shown in diagram f. Make 20 blocks.

MAKING THE QUILT
Lay out the blocks interspacing with the sashing strips and sashing posts as shown in the quilt assembly diagram. Join into 11 rows, then join the rows to complete the quilt centre. Add the side borders to the quilt centre, then join a corner post to each end of the top and bottom borders and join to the top and bottom to complete the quilt.

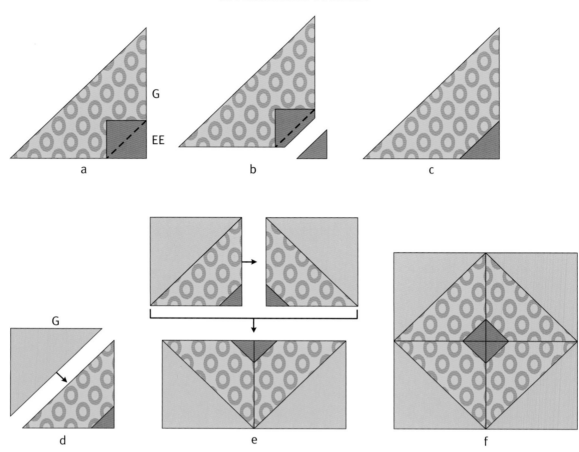

a   b   c

d   e   f

FINISHING THE QUILT

Press the quilt top. Seam the backing pieces using a ¼in (6mm) seam allowance to form a piece approx. 77in x 91in (195.5cm x 231.25cm). Layer the quilt top, batting and backing and baste together (see page 140). Using toning machine quilting stitch in the ditch throughout the quilt. Trim the quilt edges and attach the binding (see page 141).

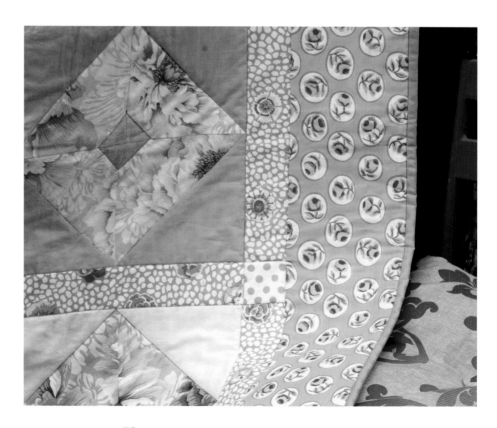

QUILT ASSEMBLY DIAGRAM

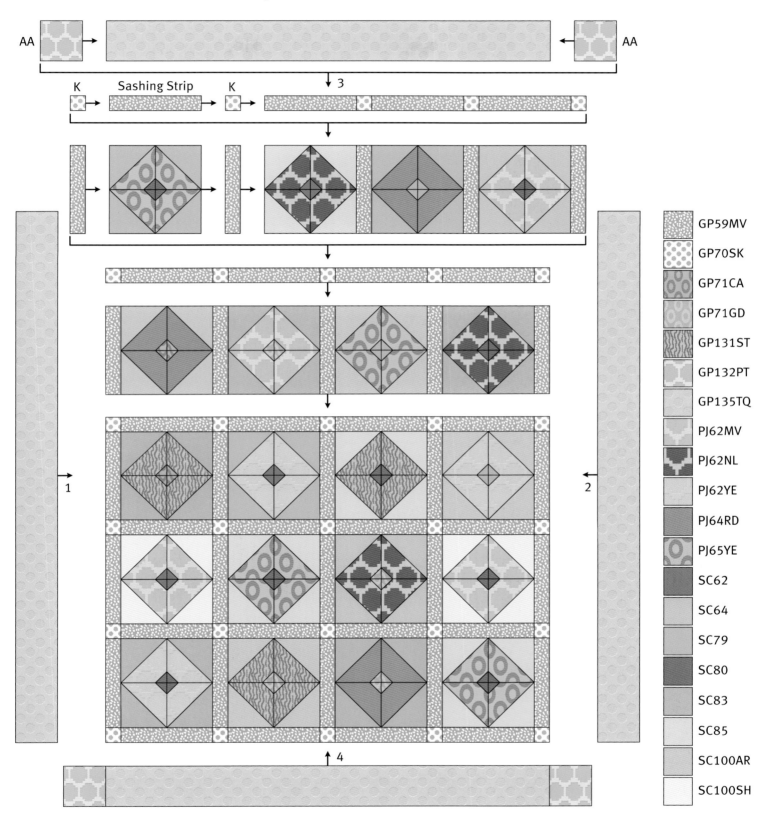

GP59MV
GP70SK
GP71CA
GP71GD
GP131ST
GP132PT
GP135TQ
PJ62MV
PJ62NL
PJ62YE
PJ64RD
PJ65YE
SC62
SC64
SC79
SC80
SC83
SC85
SC100AR
SC100SH

rouge *

Kaffe Fassett

The centre of this very straightforward quilt is made using a single square which is cut to size, no template is provided. The centre is surrounded with a simple border.

SIZE OF QUILT
The finished quilt will measure approx. 66in x 88in (167.5cm x 223.5cm).

MATERIALS
Patchwork Fabrics
CRACKLE		
Ochre	BM39OC	⅜yd (35cm)
Red	BM39RD	⅜yd (35cm)
ZIGZAG		
Warm	BM43WM	⅝yd (60cm)
GUINEA FLOWER		
Pink	GP59PK	¼yd (25cm)
ASIAN CIRCLES		
Tomato	GP89TM	⅜yd (35cm)
BIG BLOOMS		
Red	GP91RD	¼yd (25cm)
Turquoise	GP91TQ	⅜yd (35cm)
PEKING		
Red	GP130RD	⅜yd (35cm)
JUPITER		
Red	GP131RD	⅜yd (35cm)
CAMELLIA		
Pink	GP132PK	⅜yd (35cm)
BELLE EPOCH		
Red	GP133RD	⅜yd (35cm)
FLAME STRIPE		
Brown	GP134BR	⅜yd (35cm)
Red	GP134RD	¼yd (25cm)
SURREY		
Black	GP135BK	¾yd (70cm)
RIBBON STRIPE		
Red	GP137RD	¼yd (25cm)
BOUFFANT		
Red	PJ61RD	¼yd (25cm)
BROCADE PEONY		
Red	PJ62RD	⅜yd (35cm)
LAVINIA		
Red	PJ64RD	¼yd (25cm)

Border Fabric
OMBRE		
Green	GP117GN	1½yd (1.4m)

Backing Fabric 5¾yd (5.3m)
We suggest these fabrics for backing
BROCADE PEONY Red, PJ62RD
BIG BLOOMS Turquoise, GP91TQ

Binding
GUINEA FLOWER		
Apricot	GP59AP	⅝yd (60cm)

Batting
74in x 96in (188cm x 243.75cm)

Quilting thread
Toning machine quilting thread.

CUTTING OUT
Borders Cut 8 strips 6in (15.25cm) wide across the width of the fabric. Join as necessary and cut 2 borders 77½in x 6in (196.75cm x 15.25cm) for the quilt sides and 2 borders 66½in x 6in (169cm x 15.25cm) for the quilt top and bottom in GP117GN.

Squares Cut 6in (15.25cm) strips across the width of the fabric. Each strip will give you 6 squares per full width. Cut 6in (15.25cm) squares. Cut 13 in BM43WM, 12 in GP134BR, 11 in PJ62RD, 10 in GP91TQ, 9 in GP89TM, GP132PK, 7 in BM39OC, BM39RD, GP130RD, GP131RD, GP133RD, 6 in GP59PK, GP134RD, GP135BK, GP137RD, PJ61RD, PJ64RD and 5 in GP91RD. Total 140 squares.

Binding Cut 8 strips 2½in (6.5cm) wide across the width of the fabric in GP59AP.

Backing Cut 1 piece 40in x 96in (101.5cm x 243.75cm) and 1 piece 35in x 96in (89cm x 243.75cm) in backing fabric.

MAKING THE QUILT
Use a ¼in (6mm) seam allowance throughout. Refer to the quilt assembly diagram for fabric placement. Lay out all the squares as shown in the quilt assembly diagram. Join the squares into 14 rows of 10 squares. Join the rows, pressing the seam allowances in opposite directions for each row, to complete the quilt centre.

ADDING THE BORDERS
Add the side borders to the quilt centre, then join the top and bottom borders to the centre as shown in the quilt assembly diagram to complete the quilt.

FINISHING THE QUILT
Press the quilt top. Seam the backing pieces using a ¼in (6mm) seam allowance to form a piece approx. 74in x 96in (188cm x 243.75cm). Layer the quilt top, batting and backing and baste together (see page 140). Using toning machine quilting thread stitch in the ditch throughout the quilt. Trim the quilt edges and attach the binding (see page 141).

QUILT ASSEMBLY DIAGRAM

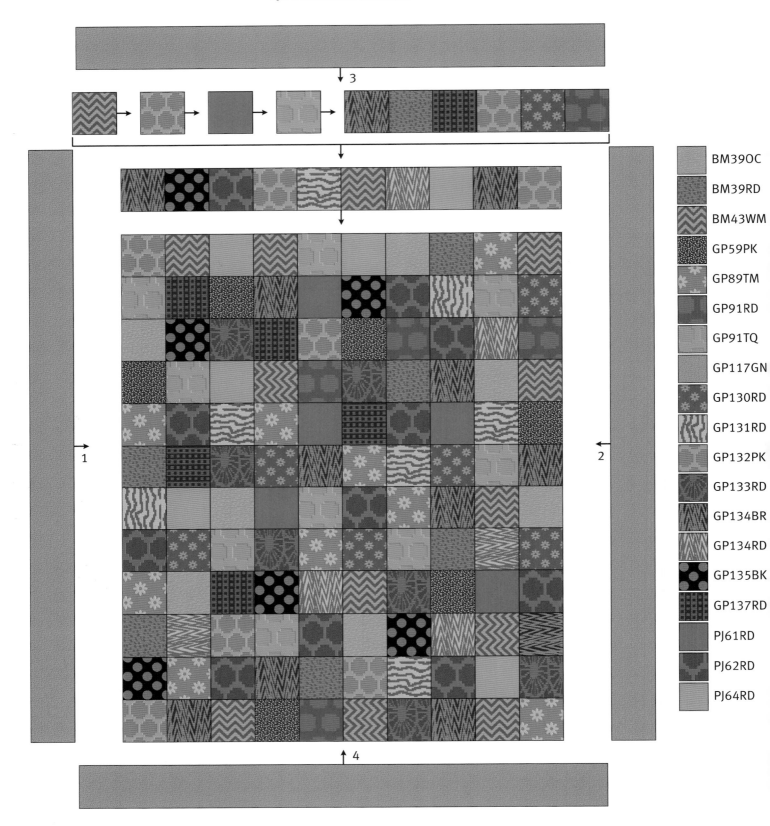

BM39OC
BM39RD
BM43WM
GP59PK
GP89TM
GP91RD
GP91TQ
GP117GN
GP130RD
GP131RD
GP132PK
GP133RD
GP134BR
GP134RD
GP135BK
GP137RD
PJ61RD
PJ62RD
PJ64RD

even weave **

Liza Prior Lucy

This simple layout is given an impressive woven effect by the clever use of Kaffe's woven stripe fabrics. A single square (Template A) is set on point in diagonal rows where the striped fabrics are alternated. The edges and corners of the quilt are completed with 2 triangles (Templates G and R).

SIZE OF QUILT
The finished quilt will measure approx. 76¼in x 76¼in (193.75cm x 193.75cm).

MATERIALS
Patchwork Fabrics
SHOT COTTON
Granite	SC66	¾yd (70cm)

WOVEN ALTERNATING STRIPE
Blue	WAS BL	½yd (45cm)
Grass	WAS GS	½yd (45cm)
Teal	WAS TE	⅝yd (60cm)

WOVEN BROAD STRIPE
Blue	WBS BL	⅝yd (60cm)
Subterranean	WBS SA	½yd (45cm)

WOVEN CATERPILLAR STRIPE
Aqua	WCS AQ	½yd (45cm)
Sprout	WCS SR	½yd (45cm)

WOVEN EXOTIC STRIPE
Emerald	WES EM	⅝yd (60cm)
Mallard	WES ML	⅝yd (60cm)

WOVEN MULTI STRIPE
Deepsea	WMS DS	⅝yd (60cm)
Lime	WMS LM	½yd (45cm)

WOVEN NARROW STRIPE
Spring	WNS SP	½yd (45cm)

Backing Fabric 5⅜yd (4.9m)
We suggest these fabrics for backing
WOVEN BROAD STRIPE Blue. WBS BL
WOVEN MULTI STRIPE Deepsea, WMS DS

Binding
WOVEN BROAD STRIPE
Blue	WBS BL	⅝yd (60cm)

Batting
84in x 84in (213.25cm x 213.25cm)

Quilting thread
Deep mauve machine quilting thread.

Templates

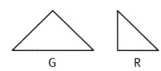

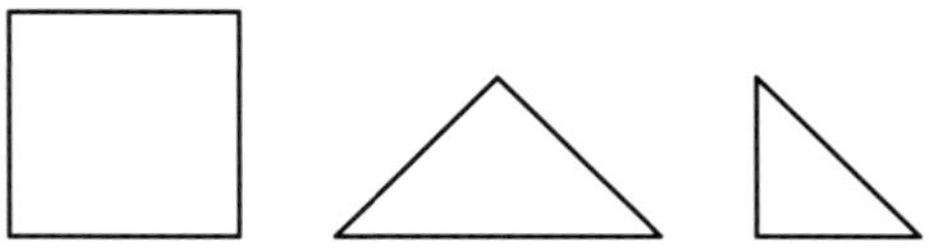

A   G   R

CUTTING OUT
Template A Cut 6½in (16.5cm) strips across the width of the fabric. Each strip will give you 6 squares per full width. Cut 15 in WAS TE, 14 in WBS BL, WES EM, 13 in WES ML, WMS DS, 12 in WAS BL, WAS GS, 11 in WCS AQ, WNS SP, 10 in WBS SA, WCS SR and WMS LM. Total 145 squares.
Template G Cut 2 strips 9¾in (24.75cm) wide across the width of the fabric in SC66. Each strip will give you 16 triangles per full width. Cut 8 squares 9¾in x 9¾in (24.75cm x 24.75cm), cut each square twice diagonally to form 4 triangles using the template as a guide, this will ensure that the long side of the triangle will not have a bias edge. Do not move the patches until both the diagonals have been cut. Cut 32 triangles in SC66.
Template R Cut a 5⅛in (13cm) strip across the width of the fabric in SC66. Cut 2 squares 5⅛in x 5⅛in (13cm x 13cm), cut each square diagonally to form 2 triangles. Cut 4 triangles in SC66.

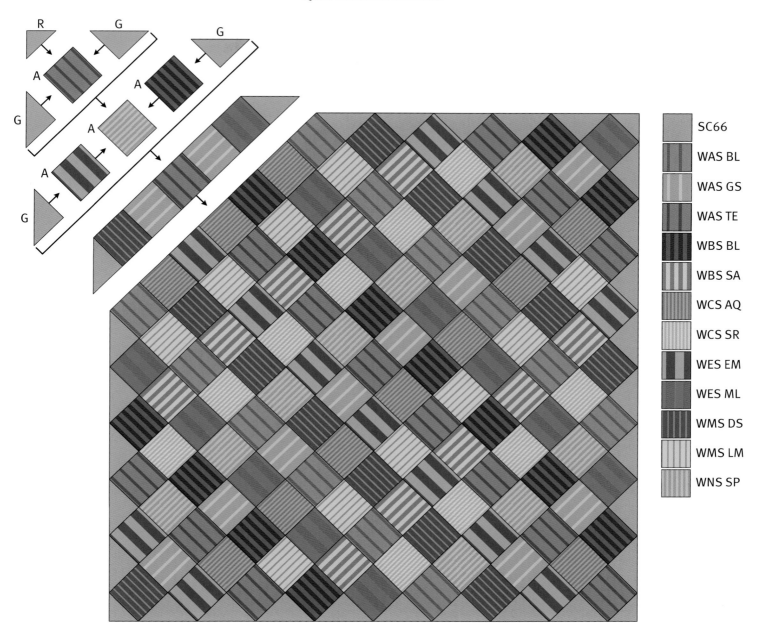

	SC66
	WAS BL
	WAS GS
	WAS TE
	WBS BL
	WBS SA
	WCS AQ
	WCS SR
	WES EM
	WES ML
	WMS DS
	WMS LM
	WNS SP

Binding Cut 8 strips 2½in (6.5cm) wide across the width of the fabric in WBS BL.

Backing Cut 2 pieces 40in x 84in (101.5cm x 213.25cm), 2 pieces 40in x 5in (101.5cm x 12.75cm) and 1 piece 5in x 5in (12.75cm x 12.75cm) in backing fabric.

MAKING THE QUILT
Use a ¼in (6mm) seam allowance throughout. Refer to the quilt assembly diagram for fabric placement and stripe direction. Lay out the squares on a design wall as shown in the quilt assembly diagram arranging the stripe directions carefully to create the woven effect. Fill in the sides with the template G triangles and the corners with the template R triangles. Carefully separate into diagonal rows and piece as shown in the quilt assembly diagram. Join the rows to complete the quilt.

FINISHING THE QUILT
Press the quilt top. Seam the backing pieces using a ¼in (6mm) seam allowance to form a piece approx. 84in x 84in (213.25cm x 213.25cm). Layer the quilt top, batting and backing and baste together (see page 140). Using deep mauve machine quilting thread quilt wavy lines parallel to the stripes in each block to enhance the woven effect. Trim the quilt edges and attach the binding (see page 141).

spice mountain ***

Liza Prior Lucy

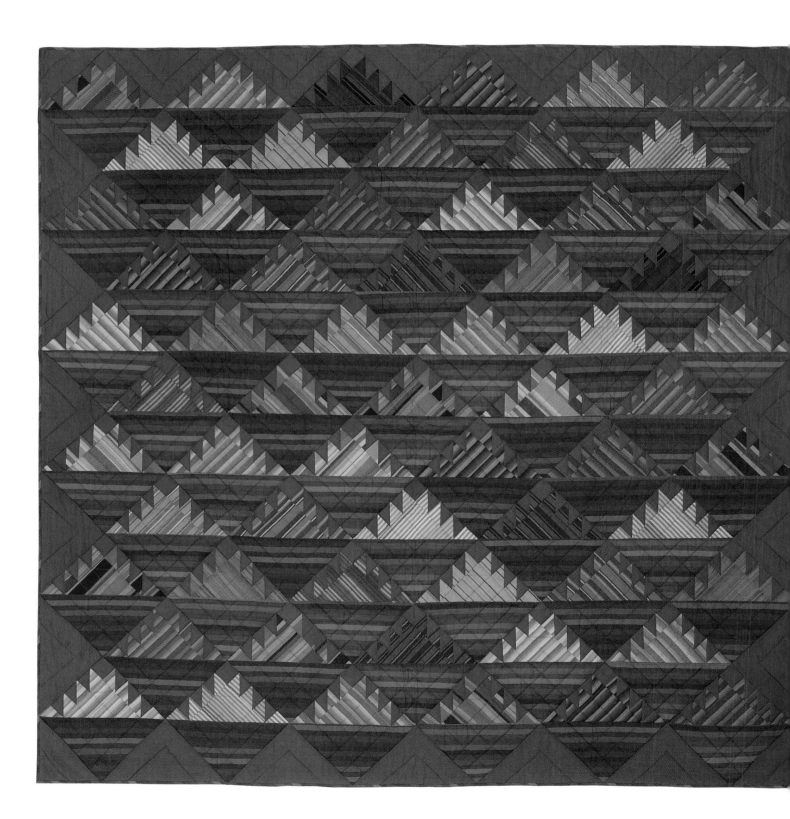

This rich quilt is made using the traditional 'Delectable Mountains' block. The blocks finish to 10in (25.5cm) square and are pieced using a square (Template K) and 2 triangles (Templates G and M), a 3rd triangle (Template OO) completes the block and is cut so that the stripes run horizontally. You'll find half template OO on page 134. Take a large piece of paper, fold, place the edge of template OO to the fold of paper, trace around shape and cut out. Open out for the complete template. Template OO is used again to fill the quilt edges and one more triangle (Template PP) is used to complete the quilt corners.

SIZE OF QUILT
The finished quilt will measure approx. 85in x 85in (216cm x 216cm).

MATERIALS
Patchwork Fabrics
SHOT COTTON

Steel	SC75	3yd (2.75m)

WOVEN ALTERNATING STRIPE

Grass	WAS GR	¼yd (25cm)
Khaki	WAS KH	¼yd (25cm)
Lavender	WAS LV	¼yd (25cm)
Orange	WAS OR	¼yd (25cm)

WOVEN BROAD STRIPE

Blue	WBS BL	3¼yd (3m)

WOVEN CATERPILLAR STRIPE

Sprout	WCS SR	¼yd (25cm)
Sunshine	WCS SU	¼yd (25cm)
Tomato	WCS TM	¼yd (25cm)

WOVEN EXOTIC STRIPE

Earth	WES ER	¼yd (25cm)
Parma	WES PM	¼yd (25cm)

WOVEN MULTI STRIPE

Deepsea	WMS DS	¼yd (25cm)
Kindling	WMS KL	¼yd (25cm)
Lime	WMS LM	¼yd (25cm)
Pimento	WMS PI	¼yd (25cm)
Raspberry	WMS RS	¼yd (25cm)
Toast	WMS TT	¼yd (25cm)

WOVEN ROMAN STRIPE

Arizona	WRS AR	¼yd (25cm)
Blood Orange	WRS BN	¼yd (25cm)
Moss	WRS MS	¼yd (25cm)

Backing Fabric 6¾yd (6.2m)
We suggest these fabrics for backing
MILLEFIORE Orange, GP92OR
WOVEN EXOTIC STRIPE Earth, WAS ER

Binding
WOVEN BROAD STRIPE

Blue	WBS BL	¾yd (70cm)

Batting
93in x 93in (236.25cm x 236.25cm)

Quilting thread
Deep grey machine quilting thread.

Templates

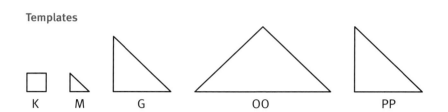

K   M   G   OO   PP

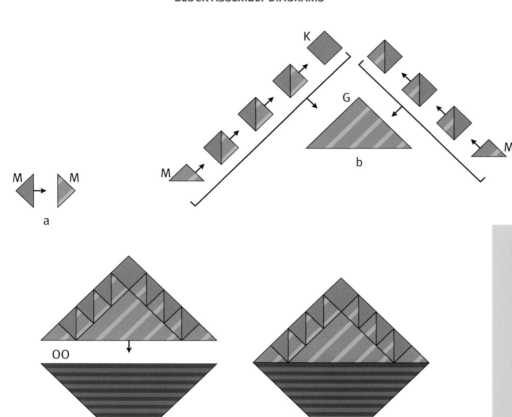

Liza says:
I highly recommend pressing all the fabrics using a generous amount of spray starch as it makes cutting and piecing much easier. Also, this is a scrappy quilt and it is not necessary to place each and every stripe in the block tops exactly as the original, just make sure that the stripes in the template G and M triangles run the same way in each block.

CUTTING OUT

Cut the fabric in the order stated to prevent waste. Be sure to pay attention to the grain lines indicated on the templates. The Woven Broad Stripe WBS BL fabric is cut so the stripes run horizontally, all other stripes run diagonally.

Template OO For fabric WBS BL cut 5 strips 7⅝in (19.25cm) wide down the length of the fabric, this will ensure that the stripes will run horizontally across the triangles. Cut 61 triangles in WBS BL. For fabric SC75 cut 7⅝in (19.25cm) strips across the width of the fabric. Each strip will give you 4 triangles per full width. Cut 20 in SC75.

Template PP Cut 2 squares 8in x 8in (20.25cm) in SC75. Cut each square diagonally to form 2 triangles using the template as a guide. Total 4 triangles.

Template K Cut 2½in (6.25cm) strips across the width of the fabric, each strip will give you 16 squares per full width. Cut 61 in SC75.

Template G Cut 6⅞in (17.5cm) strips across the width of the fabric. Cut 4 in WAS LV, WES ER, WMS DS, WMS LM, WMS PI, WMS RS, WRS AR, WRS BN, WRS MS, 3 in WAS GR, WAS KH, WCS SR, WCS SU, WCS TM, WMS KL, WMS TT, 2 in WAS OR and WES PM. Total 61 triangles. Reserve leftover strips and trim for template M.

Template M Cut 2⅞in (7.25cm) strips across the width of the fabric. Each strip will give you 26 triangles per full width. Cut 366 in SC75, 32 in WAS LV, WES ER, WMS DS, WMS LM, WMS PI, WMS RS, WRS AR, WRS BN, WRS MS, 24 in WAS GR, WAS KH, WCS SR, WCS SU, WCS TM, WMS KL, WMS TT, 16 in WAS OR and WES PM. Total 854 triangles.

Binding Cut 9¾yd (8.9m) of 2½in (6.5cm) wide bias binding in WBS BL.

Backing Cut 2 pieces 40in x 93in (101.5cm x 236.25cm), 2 pieces 40in x 14in (101.5cm x 35.5cm) and 1 piece 14in x 14in (35.5cm x 35.5cm) in backing fabric.

MAKING THE BLOCKS

Use a ¼in (6mm) seam allowance throughout. Refer to the quilt assembly diagram for fabric placement and stripe direction. Handle the pieces for the blocks carefully as there are lots of bias edges, take extra care not to tug the pieces as they are fed through the sewing machine. Arrange all the pieces for a block, make sure the stripes in the top section all tilt in the same direction.

Start by piecing 6 squares from template M triangles as shown in block assembly diagram a. Arrange the pieced squares with 2 more template M triangles, 1 template K square and a template G

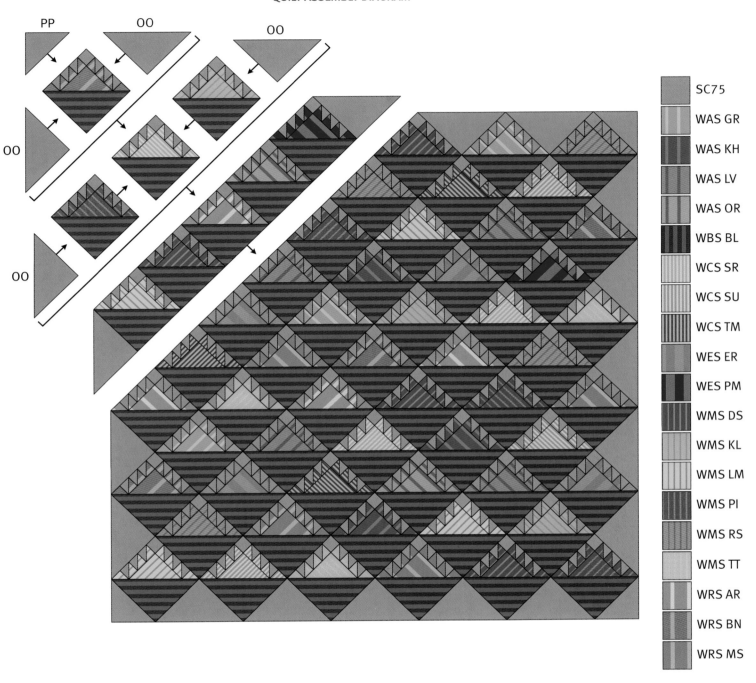

triangle as shown in diagram b. Piece as shown. Finally add the template OO triangle to complete the block as shown in diagrams c and d. Make 61 blocks.

MAKING THE QUILT
Lay out the blocks as shown in the quilt assembly diagram. Fill in the quilt sides with the template OO triangles and the corners with the template PP triangles. Carefully separate into diagonal rows and piece as shown in the quilt assembly diagram. Join the rows to complete the quilt.

FINISHING THE QUILT
Press the quilt top. Seam the backing pieces using a ¼in (6mm) seam allowance to form a piece approx. 93in x 93in (236.25cm x 236.25cm). Layer the quilt top, batting and backing and baste together (see page 140). Using deep grey machine quilting thread quilt in the ditch and then quilt additional lines as shown in the quilting diagram. Trim the quilt edges and attach the binding (see page 141).

blue morocco **

Liza Prior Lucy

The framed square in a square blocks in this graphic quilt finish to 6in (15.25cm) and use 1 square (Template L), 1 triangle (Template M) and 2 rectangles (Templates N and O). The blocks are set on point with sashing strips (Template P) with corner posts (Template Q). The edges and corners of the quilt centre are filled using 3 triangles (Templates G, R and S). The quilt centre is then surrounded with a simple border.

SIZE OF QUILT
The finished quilt will measure approx. 80in x 80in (203.25cm x 203.25cm).

MATERIALS
Patchwork and Border Fabrics
PEBBLE MOSAIC
Cobalt	BM42CB	1¼yd (1.15m)

SPOT
Pond	GP70PO	¼yd (25cm)
Sapphire	GP70SP	⅜yd (35cm)
Taupe	GP70TA	⅜yd (35m)

ABORIGINAL DOTS
Forest	GP71FO	⅜yd (35cm)
Iris	GP71IR	⅜yd (35cm)
Ochre	GP71OC	1¼yd (1.15m)
Ocean	GP71ON	⅜yd (35cm)
Purple	GP71PU	¼yd (25cm)

BELLE EPOCH
Blue	GP133BL	3⅝yd (3.3m)

Backing Fabric 6yd (5.5m)
We suggest these fabrics for backing
BELLE EPOCH Blue, GP133BL
RIBBON STRIPE Blue, GP137BL

Binding
ABORIGINAL DOTS
Periwinkle	GP71PE	¾yd (70cm)

Batting
88in x 88in (223.5cm x 223.5cm)

Quilting thread
Toning machine quilting thread.

Templates

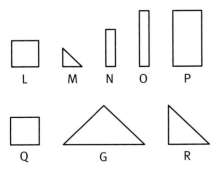

CUTTING OUT
Cut the fabrics in the order stated to prevent waste.
Borders Cut 8 strips 4½in (11.5cm) wide across the width of the fabric. Join as necessary and cut 2 borders 81½in x 4½in (207cm x 11.5cm) for the quilt sides and 2 borders 73½in x 4½in (186.75cm x 11.5cm) for the quilt top and bottom in BM42CB, these are cut a little oversize and will be trimmed to fit later.
Template G Cut 2 strips 9¾in (24.75cm) wide across the width of the fabric. Each strip will give you 16 triangles per full width. Cut 5 squares 9¾in x 9¾in (24.75cm x 24.75cm), cut each square twice diagonally to form 4 triangles using the template as a guide, this will ensure that the long side of the triangle will not have a bias edge. Do not move the patches until both the diagonals have been cut. Cut 20 triangles in GP133BL. Reserve the leftover fabric and use for template R.
Template R Cut 2 squares 5⅛in x 5⅛in (13cm x 13cm), cut each square diagonally to form 2 triangles. Cut 4 triangles in GP133BL.
Template P Cut 3in (7.5cm) strips across the width of the fabric. Each strip will give you 6 rectangles per full width. Cut 6½in x 3in (16.5cm x 7.5cm) rectangles. Cut 144 in GP133BL.
Template M Cut 2⅞in (7.25cm) strips across the width of the fabric. Each strip will give you 26 triangles per full width. Cut 244 triangles in GP133BL.

Template L Cut 3⅜in (8.5cm) strips across the width of the fabric. Each strip will give you 11 squares per full width. Use the template to cut the squares in this case as the shape is very slightly less than 3⅜in (8.5cm) square. Cut 61 in GP71OC.
Template Q Cut 3in (7.5cm) strips across the width of the fabric. Each strip will give you 13 squares per full width. Cut 60 in GP71OC.
Template S Cut 1 strip 4¾in (12cm) wide across the width of the fabric. Cut 6 squares 4¾in x 4¾in (12cm x 12cm), cut each square twice diagonally to form 4 triangles using the template as a guide, this will ensure that the long side of the triangle will not have a bias edge. Do not move the patches until both the diagonals have been cut. Cut 24 triangles in GP71OC.
Template N Cut 1½in (3.75cm) strips across the width of the fabric. Each strip will give you 8 rectangles per full width. Cut 4½in x 1½in (11.5cm x 3.75cm) rectangles. Cut 18 in GP70SP, GP70TA, GP71FO, GP71IR, GP71ON, 16 in GP70PO and GP71PU. Total 122 rectangles.
Template O Cut 1½in (3.75cm) strips across the width of the fabric. Each strip will give you 6 rectangles per full width. Cut 6½in x 1½in (16.5cm x 3.75cm) rectangles. Cut 18 in GP70SP, GP70TA, GP71FO, GP71IR, GP71ON, 16 in GP70PO and GP71PU. Total 122 rectangles.

Binding Cut 9 strips 2½in (6.5cm) wide across the width of the fabric in GP71PE.

Backing Cut 2 pieces 40in x 88in (101.5cm x 223.5cm), 2 pieces 40in x 9in (101.5cm x 22.75cm) and 1 piece 9in x 9in (22.75cm x 22.75cm) in backing fabric.

MAKING THE BLOCKS

Use a ¼in (6mm) seam allowance throughout. Refer to the quilt assembly diagram for fabric placement. Piece a total of 61 blocks as shown in block assembly diagrams a and b, the finished block is shown in diagram c.

MAKING THE QUILT

Lay out the blocks with the sashing rectangles (template P) and squares (template Q), as shown in the quilt assembly diagram. Fill in the quilt edges with the setting triangles (templates G and S) and finally the corner triangles (template R). Join the pieces into diagonal rows, then join the rows to complete the quilt centre. Add the side borders and trim to fit exactly, then add the top and bottom borders, again trim to fit exactly to complete the quilt.

FINISHING THE QUILT

Press the quilt top. Seam the backing pieces using a ¼in (6mm) seam allowance to form a piece approx. 88in x 88in (223.5cm x 223.5cm). Layer the quilt top, batting and backing and baste together (see page 140). Using toning machine quilting thread quilt in a free motion meander across the whole surface of the quilt. Trim the quilt edges and attach the binding (see page 141).

BLOCK ASSEMBLY DIAGRAMS

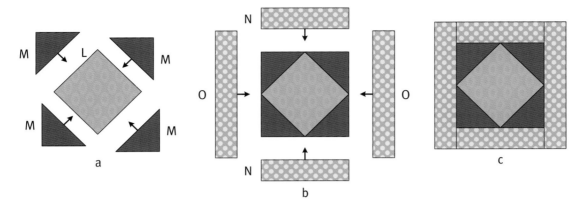

a

b

c

QUILT ASSEMBLY DIAGRAM

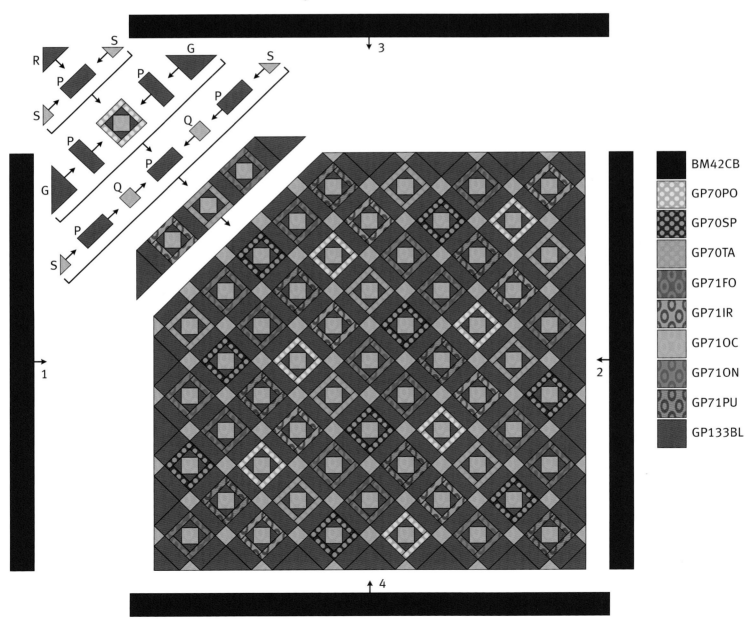

BM42CB

GP70PO

GP70SP

GP70TA

GP71FO

GP71IR

GP71OC

GP71ON

GP71PU

GP133BL

fountain **

Ruth Eglinton

This quilt features traditional sawtooth stars made with 2 squares (Template A and D) and 2 triangles (Template B and C). The blocks finish to 12in (30.5cm) square and are set in straight rows interspaced and surrounded with pieced sashing strips made using 1 square (Template E), 1 triangle (Template F) and sashing corner posts (Template D).

SIZE OF QUILT
The finished quilt will measure approx. 48in x 48in (122cm x 122cm).

MATERIALS
Patchwork Fabrics
ORIENTAL TREES
Blue   GP129BL   ¼yd (25cm)
BELLE EPOCH
Red   GP133RD   ¼yd (25cm)
GRANDIOSE
Turquoise   PJ13TQ   ¼yd (25cm)
RAMBLING ROSE
Blue   PJ34BL   ¼yd (25cm)
PETUNIAS
Green   PJ50GN   ¼yd (25cm)
PICOTTE POPPIES
Turquoise   PJ52TQ   ¼yd (25cm)
CACTUS DAHLIAS
Green   PJ54GN   ¼yd (25cm)
LAVINIA
Blue   PJ64BL   ¼yd (25cm)
Green   PJ64GN   ¼yd (25cm)
GERTRUDE
Green   PJ65GN   ¼yd (25cm)
SHOT COTTON
Aqua   SC77   2yd (1.8m)

Backing Fabric 2⅝yd (2.4m)
We suggest these fabrics for backing
WOVEN MULTI STRIPE Deep Sea, WMS DS
WOVEN CATERPILLAR STRIPE Aqua, WCS AQ
WOVEN EXOTIC STRIPE, Mallard WES MA

Binding
GERTRUDE
Green   PJ65GN   ½yd (45cm)

Batting
56in x 56in (142.25cm x 142.25cm)

Quilting thread
Dark aqua hand quilting thread

Templates

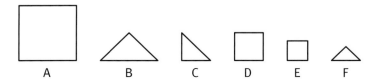

A   B   C   D   E   F

CUTTING OUT
Our usual strip cutting method is not efficient for this quilt except for the Shot Cotton background fabric, cut the fabrics in the order stated to prevent waste.
Template A Cut a 6½in (16.5cm) square from each of the following fabrics using the template as a guide. GP129BL, PJ13TQ, PJ34BL, PJ50GN, PJ52TQ, PJ54GN, PJ64BL, PJ64GN and PJ65GN. Total 9 squares.
Template C Cut 3⅞in (9.75cm) squares, cut each square diagonally to form 2 triangles. Cut 8 triangles in GP129BL, PJ13TQ, PJ34BL, PJ50GN, PJ52TQ, PJ54GN, PJ64BL, PJ64GN and PJ65GN. Total 72 triangles.
Template E Cut 2⅝in (6.75cm) squares. Cut 3 in GP129BL, PJ13TQ, PJ34BL, PJ50GN, PJ54GN, PJ64BL, 2 in PJ52TQ, PJ64GN and PJ65GN. For Shot Cotton SC77 Cut 2⅝in (6.75cm) strips across the width of the fabric, each strip will give you 15 squares per full width. Cut 48 squares in SC77. Total 72 squares.
Template F Cut 4¼in (10.75cm) squares, then using the template as a guide cut each square twice diagonally to make 4 triangles. This will ensure the long side of the triangles will not have a bias edge. Cut 7 triangles in PJ50GN, 6 in GP129BL, PJ13TQ, PJ34BL, PJ54GN, PJ64BL, 4 in PJ64GN, PJ65GN and 3 in PJ52TQ. For Shot Cotton SC77 cut 4¼in (10.75cm) strips across the width of the fabric. Each strip will give you 36 triangles per full width. Cut 4¼in (10.75cm) squares, then using the template as a guide cut each square twice diagonally to make 4 triangles. Cut 192 triangles in SC77. Total 240 triangles.

Template D Cut 3½in (9cm) strips across the width of the fabric. Each strip will give you 11 squares per full width. Cut 36 in SC77 and 16 in GP133RD. Total 52 squares.
Template B Cut 7¼in (18.5cm) strips across the width of the fabric. Each strip will give you 20 triangles per full width. Cut 7¼in (18.5cm) squares, then using the template as a guide cut each square twice diagonally to make 4 triangles. This will ensure the long side of the triangles will not have a bias edge. Cut 36 triangles in SC77.

Binding Cut 6 strips 2½in (6.5cm) wide across the width of the fabric in PJ65GN.

Backing Cut 1 piece 40in x 56in (101.5cm x 142.25cm), 1 piece 40in x 17in (101.5cm x 43.25cm) and 1 piece 17in x 17in (43.25cm x 43.25cm) in backing fabric.

MAKING THE BLOCKS AND SASHING
Use a ¼in (6mm) seam allowance throughout. Refer to the quilt assembly diagram for fabric placement. Each star is made using one print fabric. Piece a total of 9 sawtooth star blocks as shown in block assembly diagrams a and b, the finished block is shown in diagram c. Next piece 24 sashing strips as shown in diagram d, the finished strip can be seen in diagram e. Handle the sashing strips carefully as the diagonal piecing makes them a little stretchy. If you find your sashing strips come up a little small (they should measure 12½in x 3½in (31.75cm x 9cm) to the raw edge to match the star blocks) reduce your seam allowance a fraction whilst piecing the bars.

Ruth says:
Using a generous amount of spray starch on the Shot Cotton fabric to give it body makes cutting and piecing much easier.

BLOCK ASSEMBLY DIAGRAMS

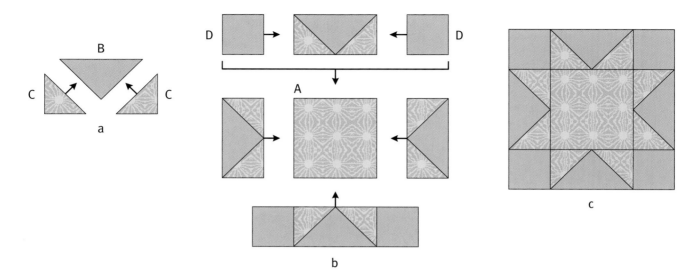

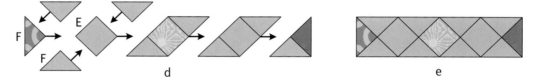

SASHING ASSEMBLY DIAGRAMS

MAKING THE QUILT
Lay out the star blocks and interspace with the pieced sashing strips and corner posts as shown in the quilt assembly diagram. Piece into 7 rows and join the rows to complete the quilt.

FINISHING THE QUILT
Press the quilt top. Seam the backing pieces using a ¼in (6mm) seam allowance to form a piece approx. 56in x 56in (142.25cm x 142.25cm). Layer the quilt top, batting and backing and baste together (see page 140). Using dark aqua hand quilting thread stitch as shown in the quilting diagram. The quilting lines are offset from the seams by ½in (1.25cm) except for the centres of the stars, where the offset is 1in (2.5cm). Trim the quilt edges and attach the binding (see page 141).

QUILTING DIAGRAM

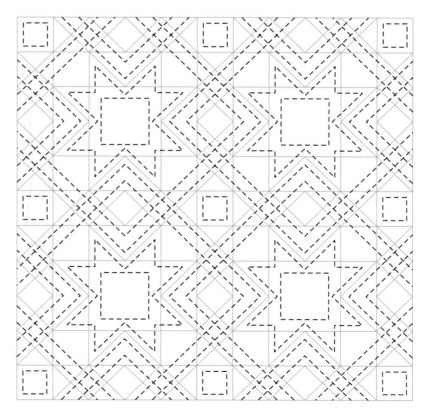

GP129BL
GP133RD
PJ13TQ
PJ34BL
PJ50GN
PJ52TQ
PJ54GN
PJ64BL
PJ64GN
PJ65GN
SC77

carnaby **

Brandon Mably

This quilt is made of 4–patch blocks which finish to 5½in (14cm) square, pieced using a square (Template BB). The 4–patch blocks are alternated with a second square (Template BB) and set 'on point' into diagonal rows. The edges and corners of the quilt are completed with 2 triangles (Templates CC and DD).

SIZE OF QUILT
The finished quilt will measure approx. 70in x 93¼in (177.75cm x 236.75cm).

MATERIALS
Patchwork Fabrics
MAD PLAID
Mauve	BM37MV	½yd (45cm)

CRACKLE
Green	BM39GN	½yd (45cm)
Grey	BM39GY	⅝yd (60cm)

JOLLY
Black	BM40BK	⅝yd (60cm)
Brown	BM40BR	⅝yd (60cm)
Grey	BM40GY	⅝yd (60cm)

POMEGRANATE
Brown	BM41BR	½yd (45cm)
Cobalt	BM41CB	¼yd (25cm)
White	BM41WH	½yd (45cm)

PEBBLE MOSAIC
Cobalt	BM42CB	½yd (45cm)
White	BM42WH	½yd (45cm)

ZIGZAG
Cool	BM43CL	½yd (45cm)
Multi	BM43MU	⅝yd (60cm)

ABORIGINAL DOTS
Olive	GP71OV	⅞yd (80cm)

UZBEKISTAN
Brown	GP136BR	⅜yd (35cm)
Grey	GP136GY	⅝yd (60cm)

Backing Fabric 6yd (5.5m)
We suggest these fabrics for backing
LOTTO Grey, BM35GY
UZBEKISTAN Grey, GP136GY

Binding
MAD PLAID
Mauve	BM37MV	¾yd (70cm)

Batting
78in x 101in (198cm x 256.5cm)

Quilting thread
Beige machine quilting thread.

Templates

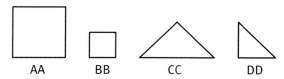

CUTTING OUT
Template AA Cut 6in (15.25cm) strips across the width of the fabric. Each strip will give you 6 squares per full width. Cut 16 in BM40BK, BM40BR, BM40GY, BM43MU, GP136GY and 8 in GP136BR. Total 88 squares.

Template BB Cut 3¼in (8.25cm) strips across the width of the fabric. Each strip will give you 12 squares per full width. Cut 72 in BM39GY, 48 in BM37MV, BM39GN, BM41BR, BM41WH, BM42CB, BM42WH, BM43CL and 24 in BM41CB. Total 432 squares.

Template CC Cut 3 strips 9in (22.75cm) wide across the width of the fabric in GP71OV. Each strip will give you 16 triangles per full width. Cut 10 squares 9in x 9in (22.75cm x 22.75cm), cut each square twice diagonally to form 4 triangles using the template as a guide, this will ensure that the long side of the triangle will not have a bias edge. Do not move the patches until both the diagonals have been cut. Total 38 triangles and 2 spare. Reserve the leftover strip and trim for template DD.

Template DD Trim the reserved strip to 4¾in (12cm) and cut 4 triangles in GP71OV.

Binding Cut 9 strips 2½in (6.5cm) wide across the width of the fabric in BM37MV.

Backing Cut 1 piece 40in x 101in (101.5cm x 256.5cm) and 1 piece 39in x 101in (99cm x 256.6cm) in backing fabric.

MAKING THE BLOCKS
Use a ¼in (6mm) seam allowance throughout. Refer to the quilt assembly diagram for fabric placement. Piece a total of 108 4–patch blocks as shown in block assembly diagram a, the finished block is shown in diagram b.

MAKING THE QUILT
Lay out the blocks alternating them with the template AA squares as shown in the quilt assembly diagram. Fill in the quilt edges with the setting triangles (templates CC) and finally the corner triangles (template DD). Join the pieces into diagonal rows, then join the rows to complete the quilt.

FINISHING THE QUILT
Press the quilt top. Seam the backing pieces using a ¼in (6mm) seam allowance to form a piece approx. 78in x 101in (198cm x 256.5cm). Layer the quilt top, batting and backing and baste together (see page 140). Using beige machine quilting thread quilt in the ditch and free motion meander across the of the quilt. Trim the quilt edges and attach the binding (see page 141).

BLOCK ASSEMBLY DIAGRAMS

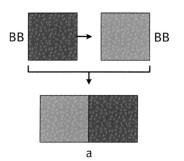

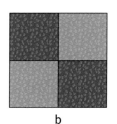

a

b

DD
CC
CC
CC
AA
CC

BM37MW
BM39GR
BM39GY
BM40BK
BM40BR
BM40GY
BM41BR
BM41CB
BM41WH
BM42CB
BM42WH
BM43ML
BM43CL
GP71OV
GP136BR
GP136GY

diamond delight ✳✳✳

Sally Davis

The bold combination of shot cottons and stripes makes a dynamic quilt! A diamond (Template SS) is used to piece 4-patch diamond centres for the main blocks. Each pieced diamond block is then framed using cut strips 'log cabin' style. Blocks with shot cotton centres are framed with stripes and blocks with stripe centres are framed with shot cottons. The blocks for the edges of the quilt are made using the diamond (Template SS) and 2 triangles (Templates TT and UU), in different combinations depending on position in the quilt, which are again framed along the inner edges.

SIZE OF QUILT
The finished quilt will measure approx. 55½in x 80in (141cm x 203.25cm).

MATERIALS
The instructions for this quilt are less formal than usual. We have included a list including most of the fabrics Sally used and suggested quantities, but these are just guidelines, this is a great opportunity to include scraps. When choosing your fabric selection, remember to include some bright 'sharp' colours to add lift.

Patchwork Fabrics
SHOT COTTON

Ginger	SC01	¼yd (25cm)
Persimmon	SC07	⅛yd (15cm)
Raspberry	SC08	⅛yd (15cm)
Bittersweet	SC10	⅛yd (15cm)
Chartreuse	SC12	¼yd (25cm)
Lavender	SC14	¼yd (25cm)
Watermelon	SC33	¼yd (25cm)
Sunshine	SC35	¼yd (25cm)
Jade	SC41	¼yd (25cm)
Lime	SC43	¼yd (25cm)
Scarlet	SC44	¼yd (25cm)
True Cobalt	SC45	¼yd (25cm)
Grape	SC47	⅛yd (15cm)
Bordeaux	SC54	¼yd (25cm)
Viridian	SC55	¼yd (25cm)
Moss	SC56	¼yd (25cm)
Brick	SC58	¼yd (25cm)
Terracotta	SC61	⅛yd (15cm)
Pool	SC71	¼yd (25cm)
Magenta	SC81	⅛yd (15cm)
Blueberry	SC88	⅛yd (15cm)
Eucalyptus	SC90	⅜yd (35cm)
Cactus	SC92	¼yd (25cm)

WOVEN ALTERNATING STRIPE

Blue	WAS BL	⅛yd (15cm)
Red	WAS RD	¼yd (25cm)

WOVEN BROAD STRIPE

Bliss	WBS BS	¼yd (25cm)
Red	WBS RD	⅛yd (15cm)
Subterranean	WBS SA	⅜yd (35cm)
Watermelon	WBS WL	⅜yd (35cm)

WOVEN CATERPILLAR STRIPE

Aqua	WCS AQ	⅜yd (35cm)
Earth	WCS ER	¼yd (25cm)
Dark	WCS DK	⅛yd (15cm)
Sprout	WCS SR	¼yd (25cm)

WOVEN EXOTIC STRIPE

Emerald	WES EM	⅜yd (35cm)
Purple	WES PU	¼yd (25cm)
Warm	WES WM	¼yd (25cm)

WOVEN NARROW STRIPE

Blue	WNS BL	¼yd (25cm)
Dusk	WNS DU	¼yd (25cm)
Heliotrope	WNS HL	¼yd (25cm)
Red	WNS RD	¼yd (25cm)
Spice	WNS SI	⅛yd (15cm)
Spring	WNS SP	⅜yd (35cm)

WOVEN ROMAN STRIPE

Dusk	WRS DU	¼yd (25cm)
Moss	WRS MS	¼yd (25cm)

Backing Fabric 4⅜yd (4m)
We suggest these fabrics for backing MILLEFIORE Blue, GP92BL or Brown, GP92BR

Binding
WOVEN EXOTIC STRIPE

Emerald	WES EM	⅝yd (60cm)

Batting
63in x 88in (160cm x 223.5cm)

Quilting thread
Toning machine quilting thread.

Templates

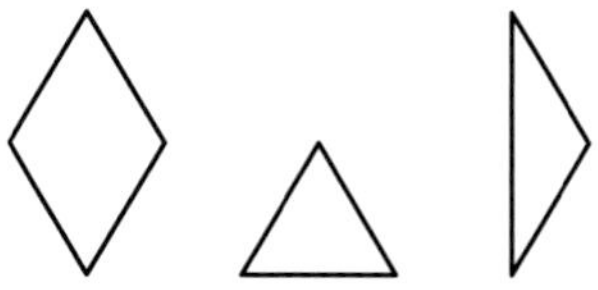

SS   TT   UU

CUTTING OUT
Cut only the shapes you need leaving the remaining fabric in the largest pieces possible. The Template SS diamonds are cut in different ways for the stripe fabrics and shot cotton fabrics.

Template SS Shot Cotton fabrics, cut 3½in (9cm) strips across the width of the fabric. Each strip will give you 9 diamonds per full width. Cut a total of 98 diamonds in shot cotton fabrics.

Template SS Stripe fabrics, cut the diamonds so that the stripes run across the width. Check the photograph for help with this. The shapes will have all bias sides, so handle very carefully. Cut a total of 120 diamonds in stripe fabrics.

Template TT Shot Cotton fabrics cut a total of 24 triangles.

Template UU Shot Cotton fabrics cut a total of 20 triangles.

Framing Strips These strips are cut 1½in (3.75cm) wide across the width of the fabric, we recommend cutting as you need these. Note that the frame around each block is pieced in the same fabric.

Binding Cut 7⅞yd (7.2m) of 2½in (6.5cm) wide bias binding in WES EM.

Backing Cut 2 pieces 40in x 63in (101.5cm x 160cm), 1 piece 40in x 9in (101.5cm x 22.75cm) and 1 piece 14in x 9in (35.5cm x 22.75cm) in backing fabric.

MAKING THE BLOCKS
Use a ¼in (6mm) seam allowance throughout. The blocks are made in 2 combinations, stripe centres with shot cotton frames (Block 1) and shot cottons centres with stripe frames (Block 2). The frame around each pieced diamond made in the same fabric. The block centres are pieced as shown in block assembly diagrams a and b. For help with piecing diamonds see the patchwork know–how section at the back on the book.

The frame around each block is added 'log cabin' style. Piece the first strip as shown in diagram c, be careful to allow enough strip so when the strip is pressed back it can be cut at an angle as shown in diagram d. Press the blocks and trim the strips to fit the raw edge of the block centre, this can be done with a rotary cutter and ruler, or use a ruler and pencil to mark the angle and cut carefully with scissors. Add the next strip as shown in

BLOCK ASSEMBLY DIAGRAMS

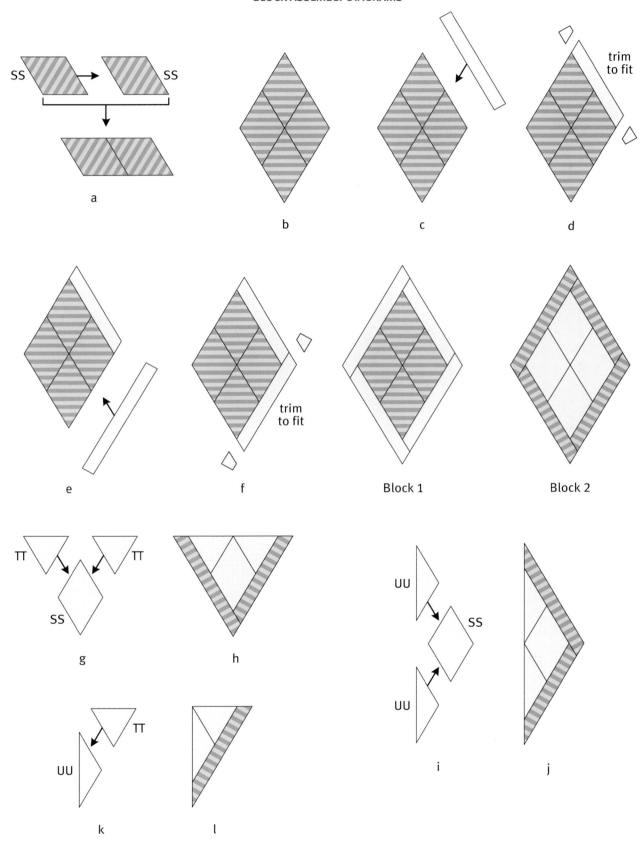

diagram e, press and trim to fit as shown in diagram f. Continue around the block in the same manner to complete the frame.

The finished blocks are shown in the diagrams titled Block 1 and Block 2. Piece 30 of Block 1 and 20 of Block 2. The edge and corner blocks all have shot cotton centres and stripe frames. These are pieced as shown in diagrams g and h, piece 10 for the top and bottom edges. Diagrams i and j, piece 8 for the side edges and finally diagrams k and l, piece 2 as shown and 2 in reverse for the quilt corners.

MAKING THE QUILT

Lay out the blocks as shown in the quilt assembly diagram. Fill in the edges with the partial blocks as shown. Carefully separate into diagonal rows and piece as shown in the quilt assembly diagram. Join the rows to complete the quilt.

FINISHING THE QUILT

Press the quilt top. Seam the backing pieces using a ¼in (6mm) seam allowance to form a piece approx. 63in x 88in (160cm x 223.5cm). Layer the quilt top, batting and backing and baste together (see page 140). Using toning machine quilting thread quilt throughout in the ditch. Then quilt each diamond as shown in the quilting diagram. Trim the quilt edges and attach the binding (see page 141).

QUILTING DIAGRAM

Shot Cottons   Stripes

teapots **

Pauline Smith

The blocks for this quilt are made using 2 rectangles (Top Rectangle and Bottom Rectangle) which are cut to size. These are pieced together to form a background for the teapot appliqué which was applied by hand using the needle–turn technique. We have provided a set of appliqué shapes (without seam allowances), but Pauline suggests you make each teapot unique as she did by varying the shapes as you sew. The blocks are stitched into straight set rows, interspaced and surrounded with sashing strips (Vertical Sashing and Horizontal Sashing) which are cut to size, and sashing posts (Template K). The quilt is completed with a simple border with corner posts (Template AA).

SIZE OF QUILT
The finished quilt will measure approx. 54¼in x 73in (137.75cm x 185.5cm).

MATERIALS
Patchwork and Border Fabrics
MAD PLAID		
Beige	BM37BE	⅞yd (80cm)
CRACKLE		
Blue	BM39BL	¼yd (25cm)
JOLLY		
Black	BM40BK	¼yd (25cm)
PAPERWEIGHT		
Purple	GP20PU	⅜yd (35cm)
SHIRT STRIPES		
Cobalt	GP51CB	⅜yd (35cm)
SPOT		
Black	GP70BK	⅓yd (30cm)
Green	GP70GN	⅜yd (35cm)
Magenta	GP70MG	⅛yd (15cm)
Sapphire	GP70SP	⅜yd (35cm)
ASIAN CIRCLES		
Dark	GP89DK	1¼yd (1.15m)
PARASOLS		
Black	GP127BK	¼yd (25cm)
PEKING		
Red	GP130RD	⅓yd (30cm)
JUPITER		
Red	GP131RD	¼yd (25cm)
PAINTED DAISIES		
Magenta	PJ35MG	⅓yd (30cm)
PICOTTE POPPIES		
Turquoise	PJ52TQ	¼yd (25cm)
SHOT COTTON		
Persimmon	SC07	⅛yd (15cm)
True Cobalt	SC45	⅛yd (15cm)
Lipstick	SC82	⅓yd (30cm)

Backing Fabric 3¾yd (3.4m)
We suggest these fabrics for backing
SHIRT STRIPES Cobalt, GP51CB
RIBBON STRIPE Blue, GP137BL

Binding
PAINTED DAISIES
Magenta   PJ35MG   ⅝yd (60cm)

Batting
62in x 80in (157.5cm x 203.25cm)

Quilting thread
Toning perlé embroidery threads.

Templates
The Appliqué Shapes for this quilt are printed on page 137.

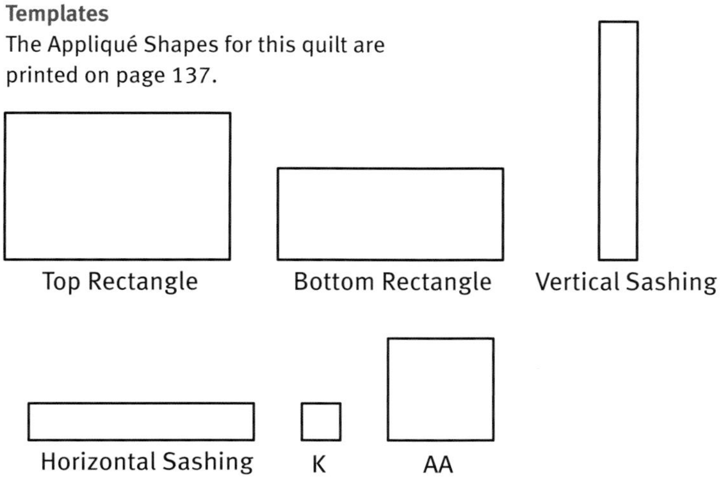

Top Rectangle   Bottom Rectangle   Vertical Sashing

Horizontal Sashing   K   AA

CUTTING OUT
We recommend drawing out the rectangles and appliqué shapes onto the fabric before cutting for the best fit and to prevent waste.

Border Cut 6 strips 6in (15.25cm) wide across the width of the fabric in GP89DK. Join as necessary and cut 2 borders 62½in x 6in (158.75cm x 15.25cm) for the quilt sides and 2 borders 43¾in x 6in (111.25cm x 15.25cm) for the quilt top and bottom.

Template AA Cut a 6in (15.25cm) strip across the width of the fabric in GP70GN. Cut 4 squares 6in x 6in (15.25cm x 15.25cm) for the border corner posts. Reserve the remaining fabric for appliqué shapes.

Top Rectangle Cut 12¼in x 8½in (31cm x 21.5cm) rectangles. Cut 4 in GP70SP, 3 in GP70BK, GP130RD and 2 in SC82. Total 12 rectangles.

Bottom Rectangle Cut 12¼in x 5½in (31cm x 14cm) rectangles. Cut 4 in GP20PU, GP51CB, 2 in BM39BL and BM40BK. Total 12 rectangles.

Vertical Sashing Cut 13½in x 2½in (34.25cm x 6.25cm) strips, cut 16 in BM37BE.

Horizontal Sashing Cut 12¼in x 2½in (31cm x 6.25cm) strips, cut 15 in BM37BE.

Template K Cut 2½in (6.25cm) strips across the width of the fabric, each strip will give you 16 squares per full width. Cut 20 squares 2½in x 2½in (6.25cm x 6.25cm) in GP70GN.

Appliqué Shapes Draw around each shape on the right side of the fabric with a washable marker leaving a space between each shape for the seam allowance. Cut the shapes adding a ¼in (6mm) seam allowance by eye. We have drawn underlaps where the shapes are layered.

Pot, Spout and Handle sets Cut 3 in GP127BK, GP131RD, PJ35MG and PJ52TQ.

Lid Cut 7 in GP70MG, 4 in GP70GN and 1 in PJ52TQ.

Knob Cut 7 in SC07 and 5 in SC45.

Binding Cut 7 strips 2½in (6.5cm) wide across the width of the fabric in PJ35MG.

Backing Cut 2 pieces 40in x 62in (101.5cm x 157.5cm) in backing fabric.

BLOCK ASSEMBLY DIAGRAMS

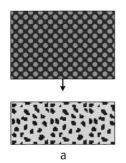

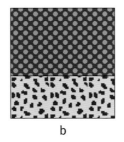

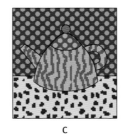

a

b

c

MAKING THE BLOCKS

Use a ¼in (6mm) seam allowance throughout. Refer to the quilt assembly diagram for fabric placement. Piece the top and bottom rectangles to form 12 background blocks as shown in block assembly diagrams a and b. Working on your first block arrange the appliqué shapes as shown in diagram c. Pin the shapes into place layering the pot over the spout and handle. Appliqué the spout and handle into place using the needle–turn technique. Next stitch the pot into place, leaving the top edge free as this will underlap the lid. Add the lid and finally the knob. Make 12 blocks.

MAKING THE QUILT

Lay out the blocks in 4 rows of 3 blocks, interspace with the vertical and horizontal sashing strips, using the template K sashing posts at the intersections as shown in the quilt assembly diagram. Separate into rows and join. Join the rows to complete the quilt centre. Add the side outer borders to the quilt centre, join a corner post to each end of the top and bottom outer borders and join to the quilt centre to complete the quilt.

FINISHING THE QUILT

Press the quilt top. Seam the backing pieces using a ¼in (6mm) seam allowance to form a piece approx. 62in x 80in (157.5cm x 203.25cm). Layer the quilt top, batting and backing and baste together (see page 140). Using toning perlé embroidery threads quilt in the ditch around the blocks. Echo quilt ¼in (6mm) outside each teapot. Trim the quilt edges and attach the binding (see page 141).

QUILT ASSEMBLY DIAGRAM

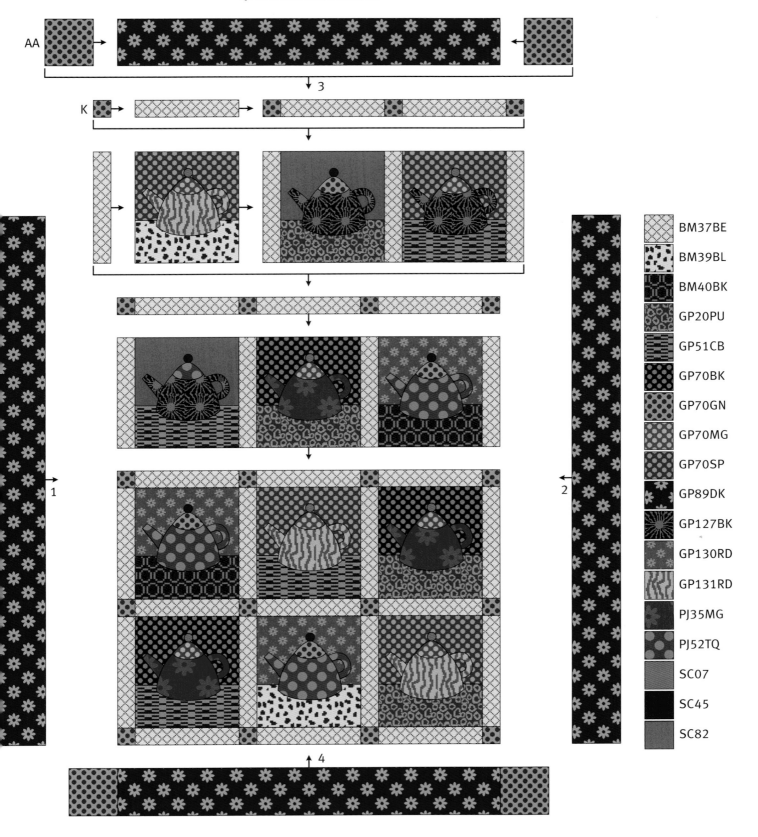

BM37BE	
BM39BL	
BM40BK	
GP20PU	
GP51CB	
GP70BK	
GP70GN	
GP70MG	
GP70SP	
GP89DK	
GP127BK	
GP130RD	
GP131RD	
PJ35MG	
PJ52TQ	
SC07	
SC45	
SC82	

mediterranean hexagons ***

Judy Baldwin

The centre of this quilt is pieced using a hexagon (Template FF) and a triangle (Template GG). This triangle is also used to make a few pieced hexagons which are cut from Ribbon Stripe fabric and form striking concentric designs dotted into the layout. Several of the fabrics are fussy cut to highlight the large blooms (and cabbages!) in the fabric designs and extra fabric has been allowed for this. The edges of the quilt centre are completed using a half hexagon (Template HH) and a second triangle (Template JJ & Reverse JJ). The quilt centre is then surrounded with a simple narrow inner border and a simple wide outer border.

SIZE OF QUILT
The finished quilt will measure approx.
80½in x 84½in (204.5cm x 214.75cm).

MATERIALS
Patchwork and Border Fabrics
ABORIGINAL DOTS

Iris	GP71IR	⅝yd (60cm)
Periwinkle	GP71PE	⅝yd (60cm)
Plum	GP71PL	1yd (90cm)

RIBBON STRIPE

Blue	GP137BL	1⅞yd (1.7m)

BRASSICA

Blue	PJ51BL	⅝yd (60cm)
Green	PJ51GN	⅝yd (60cm)

PICOTTE POPPIES

Turquoise	PJ52TQ	½yd (45cm)

CACTUS DAHLIA

Blue	PJ54BL	½yd (45cm)
Green	PJ54GN	¾yd (70cm)

BOUFFANT

Green	PJ61GN	½yd (45cm)

BROCADE PEONY

Blue	PJ62BL	1yd (90cm)
Green	PJ62GN	⅞yd (80cm)

LAVINIA

Blue	PJ64BL	½yd (45cm)
Green	PJ64GN	¾yd (70cm)

GERTRUDE

Green	PJ65GN	¾yd (70cm)

Backing Fabric 6¼yd (5.7m)
We suggest these fabrics for backing
PLINK Turquoise, GP109TQ
BRASSICA Green, PJ51GN

Binding
ABORIGINAL DOTS
Periwinkle   GP71PE   ¾yd (70cm)

Batting
88in x 92in (223.5cm x 233.75cm)

Quilting thread
Toning machine quilting thread.

Templates

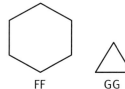 

FF   GG   HH   JJ & Rev. JJ

CUTTING OUT
Cut the fabrics in the order stated to prevent waste. We suggest cutting a template FF hexagon in clear template plastic to make selecting and fussy cutting the blooms easier. The Brassica, Cactus Dahlia and Brocade Peony fabrics are fussy cut, use the half blooms along the edges of the fabric for the template HH half hexagons shapes. The cutting instructions for cutting the Ribbon Stripe fabric, used for pieced hexagon blocks and the outer border are specific, please read the whole instruction before starting.

Template FF Fabrics PJ51BL, PJ51GN, PJ54BL, PJ54GN, PJ62BL and PJ62GN are fussy cut. Select blooms and draw around the hexagon shape with a washable pen or pencil when all the shapes are marked cut out carefully. Cut 11 in PJ62BL, 9 in PJ62GN, 7 in PJ51BL, PJ54GN, 4 in PJ51GN, 3 in PJ54BL. For the remaining fabrics cut 7in (17.75cm) strips across the width of the fabric. Each strip will give you 5 hexagons per full width. Cut 12 in PJ64GN, 11 in PJ65GN, 9 in PJ64BL, 6 in PJ52TQ, 5 in PJ10CL and PJ61GN. Total 89 hexagons. Reserve leftover fabrics for template HH.

Template HH Fussy cut 3 in PJ54GN, 2 in PJ51GN and 2 in PJ62BL. For the remaining fabrics cut 7in (17.75cm) strips and cut 2 in PJ64GN and 1 in PJ61GN. Total 10 half hexagons.

Template GG Cut 4in (10.25cm) strips across the width of the fabric. Each strip will give you 16 triangles per full width.

Cut 68 in GP71IR, GP71PE and 50 in GP71PL. Reserve leftover fabrics and trim for Template JJ & Reverse JJ. For fabric GP137BL cut a 32in (81.25cm) strip across the width of the fabric. Cut 3 strips 4in (10.25cm) wide down the length of the fabric, this will ensure the stripe direction runs correctly. Use the strips to cut 5 sets of 6 triangles as shown in block cutting and assembly diagrams a and b (you will have 1 spare set of triangles), keep the triangles together in sets of 6. Reserve the remaining fabric for the outer border. Total 216 triangles.

Template JJ and Reverse JJ Using the leftover strips from template GG cut 5 in GP71IR, 4 in GP71PE and 3 in GP71PL. Reverse the template by turning over and cut 5 in GP71IR, 4 in GP71PE and 3 in GP71PL. Total 24 triangles.

Inner Border Cut 8 strips 2in (5cm) wide across the width of the fabric in GP71PL. Join as necessary and cut 2 borders 72in x 2in (183cm x 5cm) for the quilt sides and 2 borders 71in x 2in (180.25cm x 5cm) for the quilt top and bottom.

Outer Border First take the reserved fabric from template GG. The strip should be about 28in (71cm) wide. Cut 5 strips 5½in (14cm) wide across the width in GP137BL. Also cut 5 more strips 5½in (14cm) wide across the full width of the fabric in GP137BL. Join as necessary and cut 2 borders 75in x 5½in (190.5cm x 14cm) for the quilt sides and cut 2 borders 81in x 5½in (205.75cm x 14cm) for the quilt top and bottom.

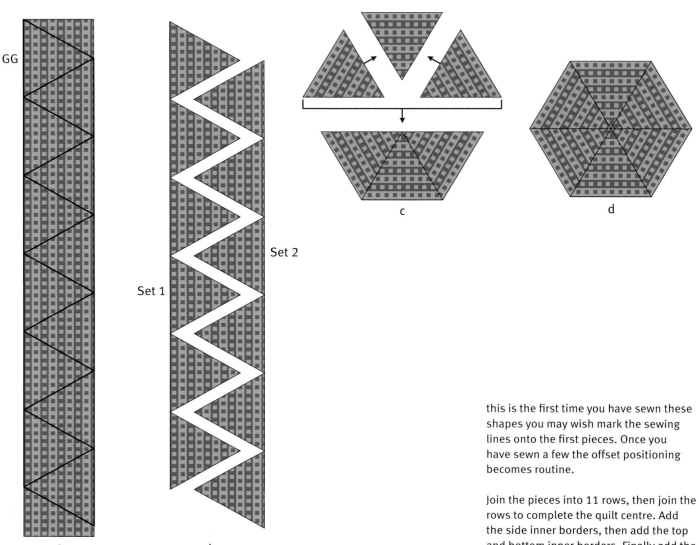

a

GG

Set 1

b

Set 2

c

d

Binding Cut 9 strips 2½in (6.5cm) wide across the width of the fabric in GP71PE.

Backing Cut 2 pieces 40in x 92in (101.5cm x 233.75cm), 2 pieces 40in x 9in (101.5cm x 22.75cm) and 1 piece 9in x 13in (22.75cm x 33cm) in backing fabric.

MAKING THE BLOCKS
Use a ¼in (6mm) seam allowance throughout. Take a set of 6 template GG triangles in GP137BL and lay them out so that the stripes form concentric circles. Join as shown in block cutting and assembly diagram c. The finished block is shown in diagram d. Make 5 blocks.

MAKING THE QUILT
Lay out the pieced blocks and template FF hexagons on a design wall referring to the quilt assembly diagram for fabric placement. Fill in the gaps with template GG triangles, you will note that these triangles form stars around the hexagons. Fill in the ends of the top and alternate rows with template JJ and Reverse JJ triangles. Fill in the ends of the second and alternate rows with template HH half hexagons, as shown in the quilt assembly diagram. To piece the first row take each hexagon and add a triangle to 2 opposite sides as shown in the diagram. When joining the pieced sections you will need to offset the sections so that the sewing lines intersect at the correct position. If

this is the first time you have sewn these shapes you may wish mark the sewing lines onto the first pieces. Once you have sewn a few the offset positioning becomes routine.

Join the pieces into 11 rows, then join the rows to complete the quilt centre. Add the side inner borders, then add the top and bottom inner borders. Finally add the side, then top and bottom outer borders to complete the quilt.

FINISHING THE QUILT
Press the quilt top. Seam the backing pieces using a ¼in (6mm) seam allowance to form a piece approx. 88in x 92in (223.5cm x 233.75cm). Layer the quilt top, batting and backing and baste together (see page 140). Using toning machine quilting thread quilt in the ditch and free motion quilt following the floral designs in the fabrics throughout the quilt centre. In the inner border quilt a free form stem and leaf design. In the outer border quilt curvy lines following alternate stripes. Refer to the photograph on page 45 for help with the design. Trim the quilt edges and attach the binding (see page 141).

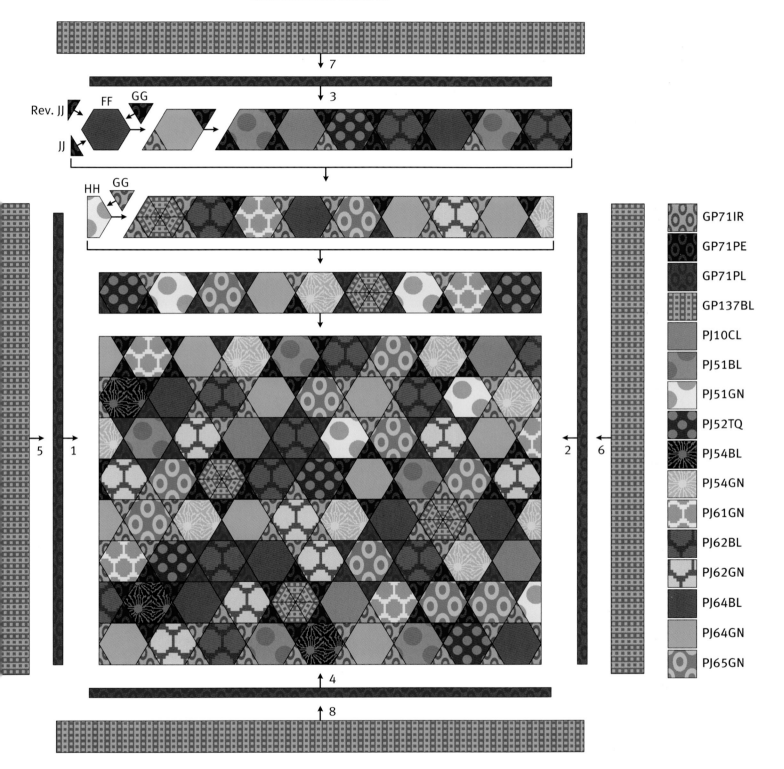

Rev. JJ
FF GG
JJ

HH GG

5 1 2 6

4

8

7

3

GP71IR
GP71PE
GP71PL
GP137BL
PJ10CL
PJ51BL
PJ51GN
PJ52TQ
PJ54BL
PJ54GN
PJ61GN
PJ62BL
PJ62GN
PJ64BL
PJ64GN
PJ65GN

mellow vintage *

Pauline Smith

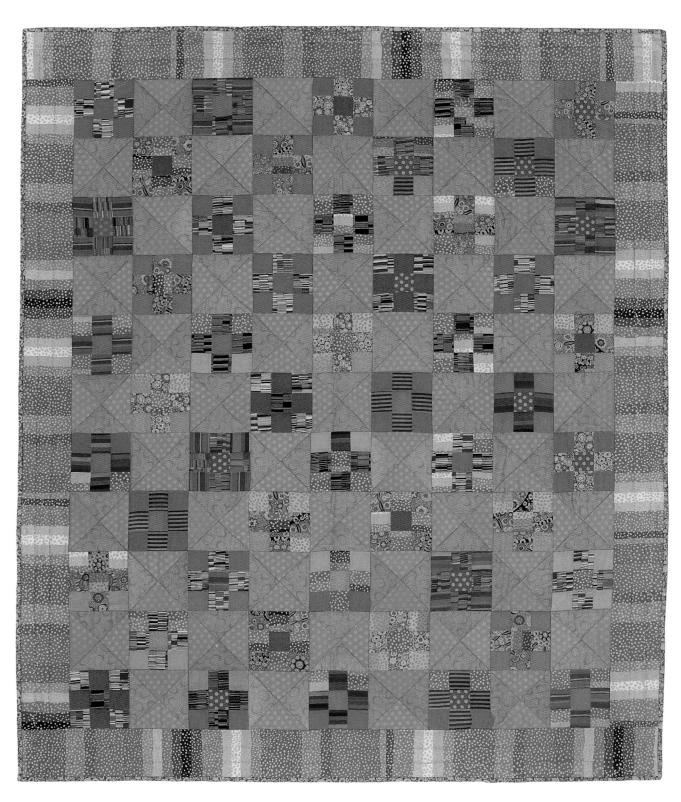

Two traditional block types which finish to 6in (15.25cm) square are combined in this gentle quilt. The first block is '9–patch', pieced using a square (Template K). The second block is 'hourglass', pieced using a triangle (Template B). The blocks are alternated throughout the quilt centre which is then surrounded with a simple border to complete the quilt. Pauline included a single square of Spot Tobacco GP70TO in the quilt, but decided that SC82 Lipstick would be just as good in the block, so that is how we have coloured the diagram and specified the fabric in the cutting and piecing instruction. If you happen to have scrap of Spot Tobacco feel free to include it if you can find the rogue square in the photograph!

SIZE OF QUILT
The finished quilt will measure approx. 64in x 71in (162.5cm x 180.5cm).

MATERIALS
Patchwork and Border Fabrics
PAPERWEIGHT		
Paprika	GP20PP	¼yd (25cm)
SHIRT STRIPES		
Brown	GP51BR	¼yd (25cm)
Cobalt	GP51CB	¼yd (25cm)
Red	GP51RD	¼yd (25cm)
SPOT		
Magenta	GP70MG	⅛yd (15cm)
Taupe	GP70TA	1¼yd (1.15m)
ABORIGINAL DOTS		
Purple	GP71PU	1¼yd (1.15m)
MILLEFIORE		
Brown	GP92BR	¼yd (25cm)
OMBRE		
Green	GP117GN	¼yd (25cm)
Purple	GP117PU	1⅝yd (1.5m)
SHOT COTTON		
Brick	SC58	⅛yd (15cm)
Magenta	SC81	¼yd (25cm)
Lipstick	SC82	¼yd (25cm)
Blueberry	SC88	¼yd (25cm)
Quartz	SC100QZ	⅛yd (15cm)
Violet	SC100VI	⅛yd (15cm)
WOVEN ALTERNATING STRIPE		
Blue	WAS BL	¼yd (25cm)
WOVEN CATERPILLAR STRIPE		
Earth	WCS ER	¼yd (25cm)
WOVEN NARROW STIPE		
Red	WNS RD	⅛yd (15cm)

Backing Fabric 4¼yd (3.9m)
We suggest these fabrics for backing
PAPERWEIGHT Paprika, GP20PP
WOVEN ALTERNATING STRIPE Blue, WAS BL

Binding
PAPERWEIGHT		
Paprika	GP20PP	⅝yd (60cm)

Batting
72in x 79in (183cm x 200.5cm)

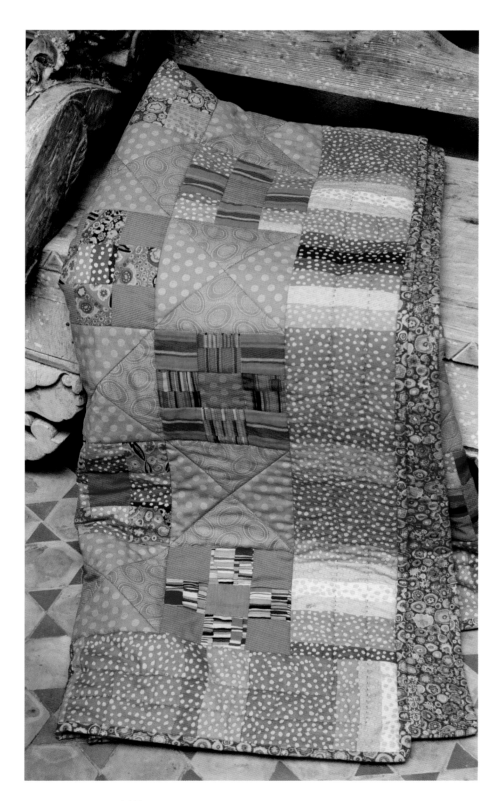

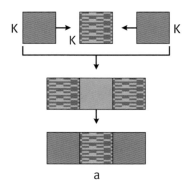
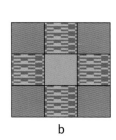
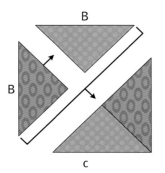
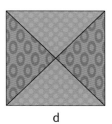

a   b   c   d

Quilting thread
Soft mauve perlé embroidery thread.

Templates

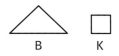

B   K

CUTTING OUT

Cut the fabrics in the order stated to prevent waste.

Borders Cut 7 strips 5½in (14cm) wide across the width of the fabric. Join as necessary and cut 2 borders 66½in x 5½in (169cm x 14cm) for the quilt sides and 2 borders 64½in x 5½in (163.75cm x 14cm) for the quilt top and bottom in GP117PU.

Template B Cut 7¼in (18.5cm) strips across the width of the fabric. Each strip will give you 20 triangles per full width. Cut 7¼in (18.5cm) squares, then using the template as a guide cut each square twice diagonally to make 4 triangles. This will ensure the long side of the triangles will not have a bias edge. Cut 98 triangles in GP70TA and GP71PU. Total 196 triangles.

Template K Cut 2½in (6.25cm) strips across the width of the fabric, each strip will give you 16 squares per full width. Cut 70 in GP117PU, 48 in GP92BR, 44 in GP51BR, 36 in SC88, 35 in GP117GN, 31 in SC82, 29 in WAS BL, 25 in GP51CB, 23 in GP51RD, 20 in GP20PP, 18 in SC81, 17 in WCS ER, 14 in SC58, 13 in WNS RD, 12 in SC100VI, 11 in GP70MG and 4 in SC100QZ. Total 450 squares.

Binding Cut 7 strips 2½in (6.5cm) wide across the width of the fabric in GP20PP.

Backing Cut 2 pieces 40in x 72in (101.5cm x 183cm) in backing fabric.

MAKING THE BLOCKS

Use a ¼in (6mm) seam allowance throughout. Refer to the quilt assembly diagram for fabric placement. Piece a total of 50 9–patch blocks as shown in block assembly diagram a, the finished 9–patch block is shown in diagram b. You will notice that the Ombre fabrics, green GP117GN and purple GP117PU have a lot of colour variation. Group the squares by colour and use similar squares for each block. Check the photograph for help with this.

Next piece 49 hourglass blocks as shown in diagram c, the finished hourglass blocks can be seen in diagram d.

MAKING THE QUILT

Lay out the 9–patch and hourglass blocks alternately as shown in the quilt assembly diagram. Piece into 11 rows of 9 blocks, join the rows to complete the quilt centre. Add the side borders, then the top and bottom borders to complete the quilt.

FINISHING THE QUILT

Press the quilt top. Seam the backing pieces using a ¼in (6mm) seam allowance to form a piece approx. 72in x 79in (183cm x 200.5cm). Layer the quilt top, batting and backing and baste together (see page 140). Using soft mauve perlé embroidery thread hand quilt in the ditch diagonally across each hourglass block, quilt around the centre square of each 9–patch block and finally quilt 2 parallel lines in the border. Trim the quilt edges and attach the binding (see page 141).

Pauline says:
Handle the template B triangles carefully as the short sides are cut on the bias, with the long sides on the straight grain. This makes sewing the diagonal seams in the block a little tricky but the finished block will be much easier to handle as the edges will be on the straight grain.

QUILT ASSEMBLY DIAGRAM

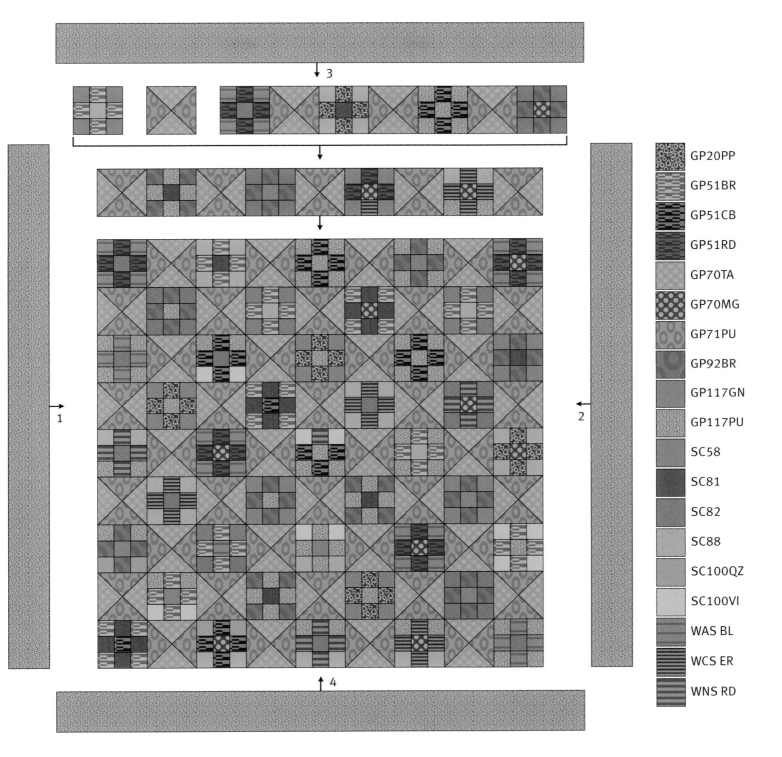

GP20PP
GP51BR
GP51CB
GP51RD
GP70TA
GP70MG
GP71PU
GP92BR
GP117GN
GP117PU
SC58
SC81
SC82
SC88
SC100QZ
SC100VI
WAS BL
WCS ER
WNS RD

jumping jupiter **

Julie Stockler

This medallion style quilt is built in layers around a central square (cut to 10in (25.5cm)), this is surrounded by triangles (Template MM). Then comes the first simple border with square corner posts (Template BB). This centre section is then set on point with the addition of triangular sections pieced using 2 triangles (Template LL and Large Triangle which is cut to size).

The second simple border with square corner posts (Template KK) is then added. The final border is pieced, made with 1 square (Template D) and 1 triangle (Template C), the ends of this section are slightly oversized and are trimmed to fit exactly, this border also has square corner posts (Template NN). Julie hand appliquéd 3 'planets' to the centre to complete the quilt.

SIZE OF QUILT
The finished quilt will measure approx. 42½in x 42½in (108cm x 108cm).

MATERIALS
Patchwork and Border Fabrics
RINGS
Robin Egg   BM15RE   ¼yd (25cm)
DANCING PAISLEY
Regal   BM22RG   ⅛yd (15cm)
POMEGRANATE
Cobalt   BM41CB   ⅛yd (15cm)
ROMAN GLASS
Purple   GP01PU   ⅛yd (15cm)
PAPERWEIGHT
Purple   GP20PU   ⅜yd (35cm)
SPOT
Green   GP70GN   ⅛yd (15cm)
Red   GP70RD   ¼yd (25cm)
Royal   GP70RY   ⅛yd (15cm)
MILLEFIORE
Blue   GP92BL   ⅜yd (35cm)
OMBRE
Blue   GP117BL   ⅝yd (60cm)
JUPITER
Multi   GP131MU   ¼yd (25cm)
FLAME STRIPE
Red   GP134RD   ½yd (45cm)
UZBEKISTAN
Red   GP136RD   ⅝yd (60cm)
RIBBON STRIPE
Blue   GP137BL   ¼yd (25cm)

Backing Fabric 2¼yd (2.1m)
We suggest these fabrics for backing
JUPITER Multi, GP131MU
UZBEKISTAN Red, GP136RD

Binding
RINGS
Robin Egg   BM15RE   ½yd (45cm)

Batting
50in x 50in (127cm x 127cm)

Quilting thread
Toning machine quilting thread.

Templates

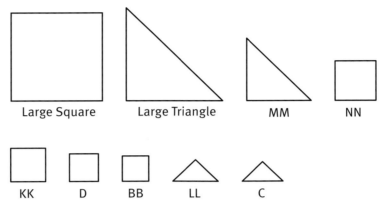

Large Square   Large Triangle   MM   NN

KK   D   BB   LL   C

CUTTING OUT
Except where stated our normal strip cutting method is not appropriate for this quilt as it would be very wasteful. Cut only the shapes you need and leave the remaining fabric in the largest pieces possible for subsequent cutting.
Large Square Cut a 10in x 10in (25.5cm x 25.5cm) in GP117BL.
Border 2 Cut 4 borders 4⅛in x 27¼in (10.5cm x 69.25cm) in GP117BL.
Large Triangle Cut 2 squares 10⅞in x 10⅞in (27.75cm x 27.75cm) in GP20PU. Cut each square diagonally to form 2 triangles. Total 4 triangles.
Template MM Fussy cut 4 triangles in GP134RD so that a blue zigzag runs from the right angle to the centre of the long side. Refer to the photograph for help with this. Total 4 triangles.
Template NN Cut 4 squares 4¾in x 4¾in (12cm x 12cm) in GP70RD.
Template KK Cut 4 squares 4⅛in x 4⅛in (10.5cm x 10.5cm) in BM15RE.
Template D Cut 3½in x 3½in (9cm x 9cm) squares. Cut 4 in BM15RE, BM22RG, BM41CB, GP70GN, GP70RY, GP92BL, GP131MU and GP137BL. Total 32 squares.
Template BB Cut 4 squares 3¼in x 3¼in (8.25cm x 8.25cm) in BM15RE.

Template LL With the straight grain running along the long side of the triangles cut 12 in GP70RD, 8 in GP01PU and GP137BL. Total 28 triangles.
Template C Cut 5½in (14cm) strips across the width of the fabric, each strip will give you 28 triangles per full strip. Cut 5½in squares, cut each square twice diagonally to form 4 triangles using the template as a guide. Do not move the pieces until both diagonals have been cut. This will ensure the long side of the triangles will not have a bias edge. Cut 72 triangles in GP136RD.
Border 1 Cut 4 borders 3¼in x 14in (8.25cm x 35.5cm) in GP92BL.
Appliqué Shapes Cut 3 circles in GP131MU at 6in, 3in and 2½ in (15.25cm, 7.5cm and 6.25cm) in diameter, a ¼in (6mm) seam allowance is included in these measurements. Julie fussy cut her circles to capture the 'Jupiter spot' in the fabric design.

Binding Cut 5 strips 2½in (6.5cm) wide across the width of the fabric in BM15RE.

Backing Cut 1 piece 40in x 50in (101.5cm x 127cm), 1 piece 40in x 11in (101.5cm x 28cm and 1 piece 11in x 11in (28cm x 28cm) in backing fabric.

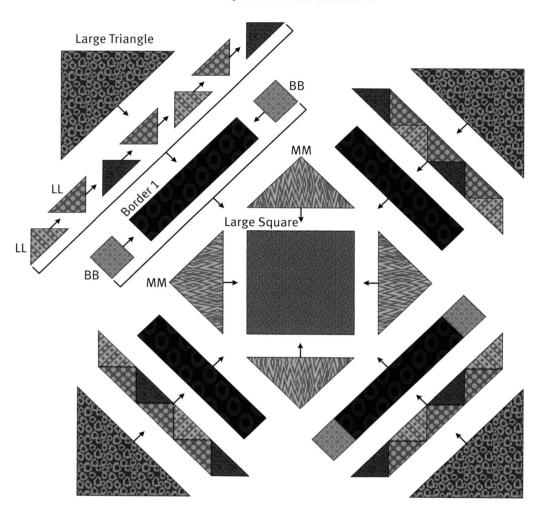

MAKING THE QUILT

Use a ¼in (6mm) seam allowance throughout and refer to the quilt assembly diagrams for fabric placement. Take the centre square and add the 4 template MM triangles as shown in quilt assembly diagram 1, when adding triangles add 2 opposite sides, press, then add the other 2 opposite sides. Add border 1 as shown.

Now is a good time to do the appliqué, prepare 3 circular card templates 5½in, 2½in and 2in (14cm, 6.25cm and 5cm) in diameter. Work a running stitch around each fabric circle close to the raw edge. Place the appropriate card circle onto each fabric circle and gather up the stitching to form a perfect fabric circle and press to set the shape, remove the card circles. Hand appliqué the fabric circles to the background as shown in quilt assembly diagram 2.

Sub-piece the next sections with template LL and large triangles as shown and add to the centre in the same manner as before. Next add border 2 as shown in quilt assembly diagram 2. Sub-piece border 3 and trim to fit exactly, then add to the centre as shown to complete the quilt.

FINISHING THE QUILT

Press the quilt top. Seam the backing pieces using a ¼in (6mm) seam allowance to form a piece approx. 50in x 50in (127cm x 127cm). Layer the quilt top, batting and backing and baste together (see page 140). Using toning machine quilting thread stitch in the ditch and then free motion meander quilt in the large shapes. Trim the quilt edges and attach the binding (see page 141).

QUILT ASSEMBLY DIAGRAM 2

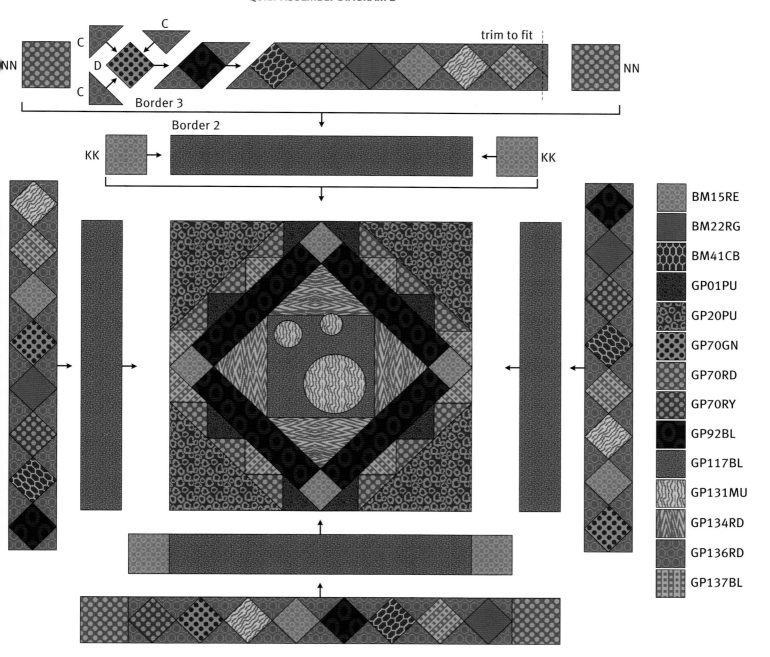

NN

C
C
D
C

Border 3

trim to fit

NN

Border 2

KK

KK

BM15RE
BM22RG
BM41CB
GP01PU
GP20PU
GP70GN
GP70RD
GP70RY
GP92BL
GP117BL
GP131MU
GP134RD
GP136RD
GP137BL

cayenne ***

Corienne Kramer

This quilt is primarily made using a square (Template VV) which is set on point. A large triangle (Template WW) is used to fill along the quilt edges and a small triangle (Template XX) is used for the quilt corners. Some of the squares are pieced using fussy cut strip sets of fabric to create a striking zigzag effect across the quilt. We strongly suggest you make clear plastic templates for this quilt as several of the fabrics are fussy cut and the templates are also used to trim pieced sections of the strip sets. Unfortunately, due to the size, the templates for this quilt are printed at 50% of true size, photocopy at 200% before using.

SIZE OF QUILT
The finished quilt will measure approx. 79¼in x 84¾in (201.25cm x 215.25cm).

MATERIALS
Patchwork and Binding Fabrics
PEBBLE MOSAIC
Orange	BM42OR	2⅜yd (2.2m)

incl. binding
ASIAN CIRCLES
Tomato	GP89TM	⅝yd (60cm)

CHARD
Hot	GP128HT	¾yd (70cm)

BELLE EPOCH
Red	GP133RD	1½yd (1.4m)

FLAME STRIPE
Brown	GP134BR	1⅝yd (1.5m)

FOXGLOVES
Hot	PJ10HT	1⅛yd (1m)

GRANDIOSE
Magenta	PJ13MG	⅝yd (60cm)

FLOATING MUMS
Red	PJ49RD	1¼yd (1.15m)

JOY
Pink	PJ60PK	1⅛yd (1m)

Backing Fabric 6⅜yd (5.8m)
We suggest these fabrics for backing
GERTRUDE Orange, PJ65OR
MILLEFIORE Red, GP92RD

Batting
87in x 93in (221cm x 236.25cm)

Quilting thread
Toning machine and/or hand quilting thread.

Templates

VV WW XX

CUTTING OUT
Cut the fabric in the order stated to prevent waste. Please read the whole instruction carefully before starting as several of the fabrics are fussy cut. We have provided a cutting layout diagram for fabrics PJ10HT and PJ60PK.

Template VV For Fabrics PJ10HT and PJ60PK refer to the cutting layout. Cut 13 squares 8½in x 8½in (21.5cm x 21.5cm) in PJ10HT and PJ60PK as shown. Handle these squares carefully as all sides are cut on the bias. For all other fabrics cut 8½in (21.5cm) strips across the width of the fabric, each strip will give you 4 squares per full width. Cut 8½in x 8½in (21.5cm x 21.5cm) squares. Cut 20 in GP133RD, 7 in PJ13MG, 6 in GP89TM and PJ49RD. Total 65 squares.

Strips for Pieced Blocks The strips are cut at 4¾in (12cm). The Flame Stripe GP134BR fabric is cut across the width. Fussy cut a total of 8 strips 4¾in (12cm) wide, 4 with dark purple zigzags and 4 with dusty purple zigzags. Try and cut each set so they are as closely matched as possible. The Pebble Mosaic BM42OR

fabric is cut down the length of the fabric with the yellow pebbles at one side of each strip, cut 8 strips 4¾in x 40in (12cm x 101.5cm). You will get 7 strips from a 40in length of fabric so you will need 2 lengths to get the 8 strips. Reserve the remaining fabric which should be approx. 35in (89cm) wide for the binding.

Template WW For Fabrics PJ10HT and PJ60PK refer to the cutting layout. Cut 2 triangles in PJ10HT and PJ60PK. For Fabric GP128HT fussy cut 7 triangles centred on the leaf bunches with long skinny stems, refer to the photograph for help with this. For the other fabrics cut 6¼in (16cm) strips across the width of the fabric, each strip will give you 5 triangles per full width. Cutting this way will ensure the long side of the triangles will not have a bias edge. Cut 8 in PJ49RD, 2 in GP89TM and GP133RD. Total 23 triangles.

Template XX Cut a 6½in (16.5cm) square in PJ49RD, cut the square diagonally to form 2 triangles.

Binding Using the reserved BM42OR fabric cut 10 strips 2½in (6.5cm) wide across the width.

Backing Cut 2 pieces 40in x 87in (101.5cm x 221cm), 2 pieces 40in x 14in (101.5cm x 35.5cm) and 1 piece 14in x 14in (35.5cm x 35.5cm) in backing fabric.

CUTTING LAYOUT FOR PJ10HT AND PJ60PK

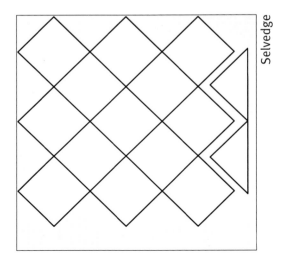

a

b

c

d

MAKING THE BLOCKS

Use a ¼in (6mm) seam allowance throughout. Refer to the quilt assembly diagram and photograph for fabric placement. Make 8 strip sets from a strip of GP134BR and a strip of BM42OR. The yellow pebbles along the edge of the BM42OR should be furthest from the GP134BR fabric. From each strip set cut 4 squares 9in x 9in (22.75cm x 22.75cm) as shown in block cutting and assembly diagram a. Keep the squares sorted by zigzag colourway (dark purple and dusty purple).

Take 2 squares of the same colourway and lay them with the BM42OR fabric at the top. Cut the first square diagonally from top left to bottom right, the second square from top right to bottom left as shown in diagram b. Using the 4 cut triangles combine them as shown in diagram b to make 2 pieced squares as shown in diagrams c and d. In the dark purple colourway make 7 squares as shown in diagram c and 6 as shown in diagram d. In the dusty purple colourway make 6 squares as shown in diagram c and 7 as shown in diagram d. Keep 4 cut triangles to fill in the quilt sides. Trim the pieced squares evenly using Template VV making sure you align the marked seam lines carefully. Also trim (if necessary) the

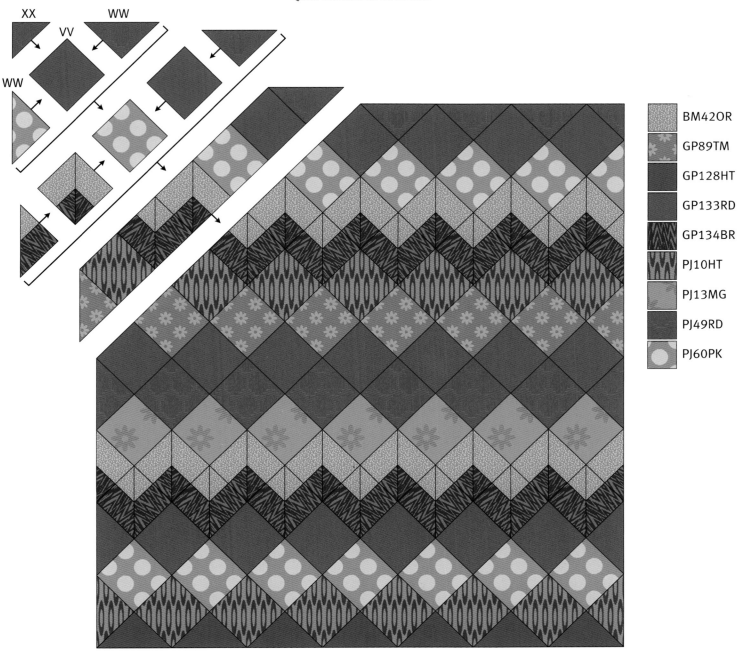

Legend:
- BM42OR
- GP89TM
- GP128HT
- GP133RD
- GP134BR
- PJ10HT
- PJ13MG
- PJ49RD
- PJ60PK

cut triangles using Template WW and stay stitch along the bias edge to stabilize.

MAKING THE QUILT
Lay out all the cut and pieced blocks in as shown in the quilt assembly diagram. Fill in the quilt sides with the template VV triangles and the top corners with the template XX triangles. Piece in diagonal rows as shown in the quilt assembly diagram.

FINISHING THE QUILT
Press the quilt top. Seam the backing pieces using a ¼in (6mm) seam allowance to form a piece approx. 87in x 93in (221cm x 236.25cm). Layer the quilt top, batting and backing and baste together (see page 140). Using toning machine quilting thread quilt in the ditch throughout the quilt, then meander quilt following the designs in the fabrics, in the zigzag rows emphasise the zigzags

in the flame stripe fabric. Trim the quilt edges and attach the binding (see page 141).

templates

Please refer to the individual instructions for the templates required for each quilt as some templates are used in several projects. The arrows on the templates should be lined up with the straight grain of the fabric, which runs either along the selvedge or at 90 degrees to the selvedge. Following the marked grain lines is important to prevent patches having bias edges along block and quilt edges which can cause distortion. In some quilts the arrows also denote stripe direction.

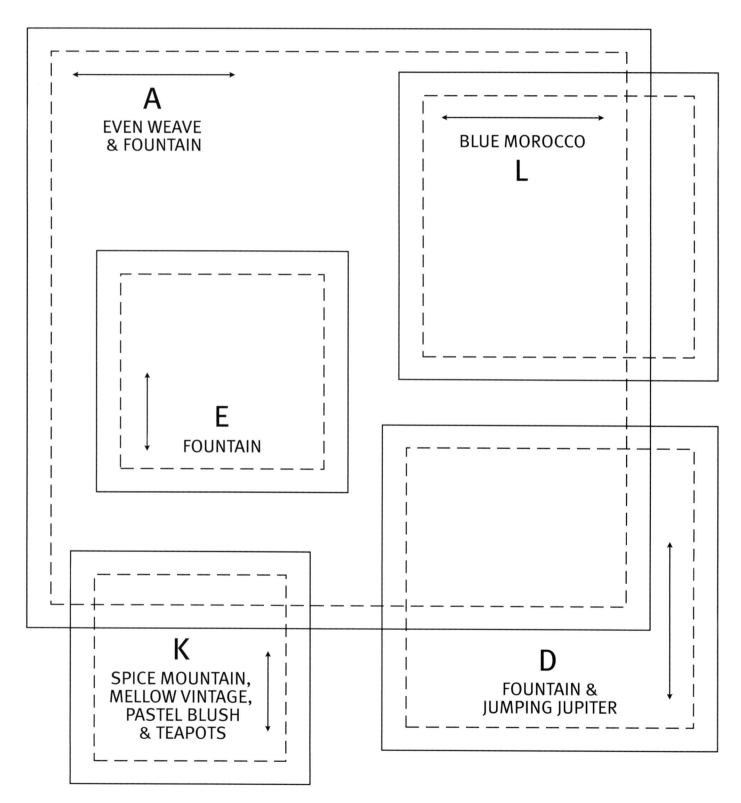

A
EVEN WEAVE
& FOUNTAIN

BLUE MOROCCO
L

E
FOUNTAIN

K
SPICE MOUNTAIN,
MELLOW VINTAGE,
PASTEL BLUSH
& TEAPOTS

D
FOUNTAIN &
JUMPING JUPITER

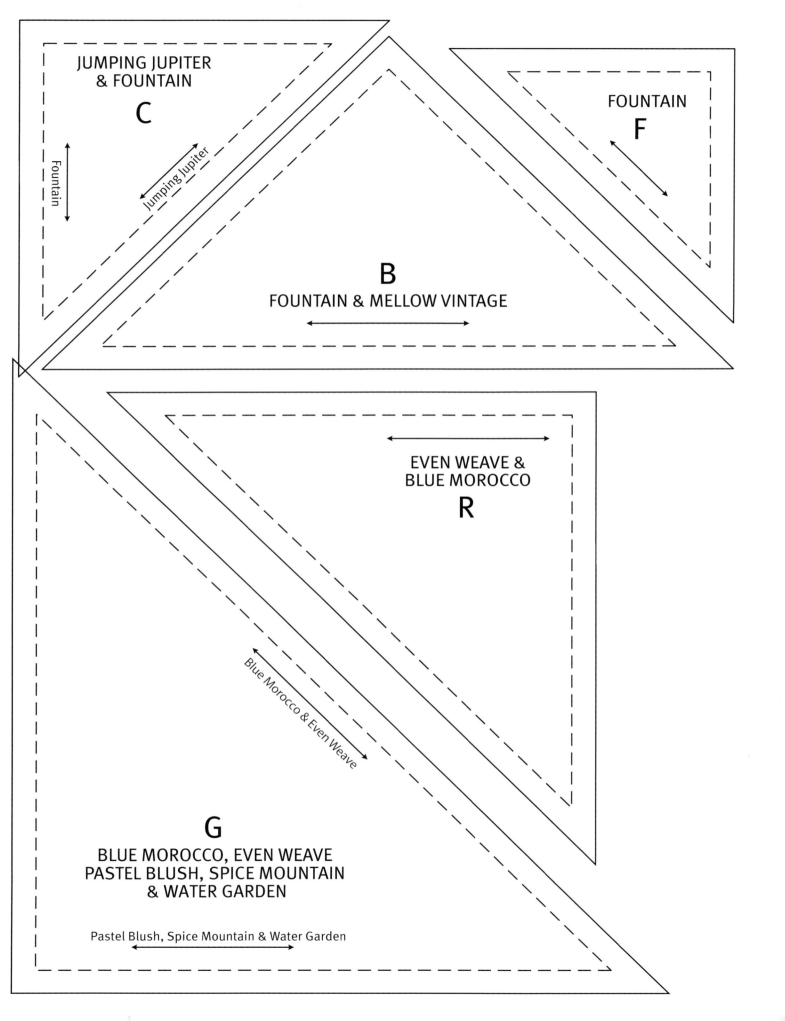

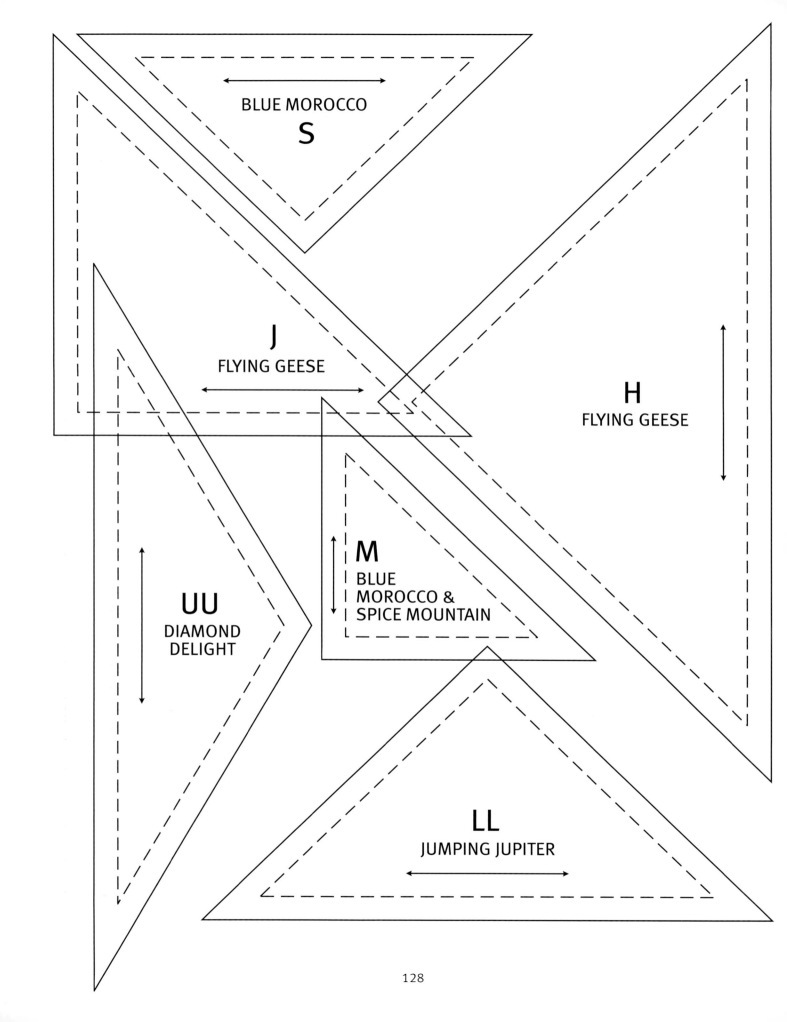

BLUE MOROCCO
S

J
FLYING GEESE

H
FLYING GEESE

M
BLUE
MOROCCO &
SPICE MOUNTAIN

UU
DIAMOND
DELIGHT

LL
JUMPING JUPITER

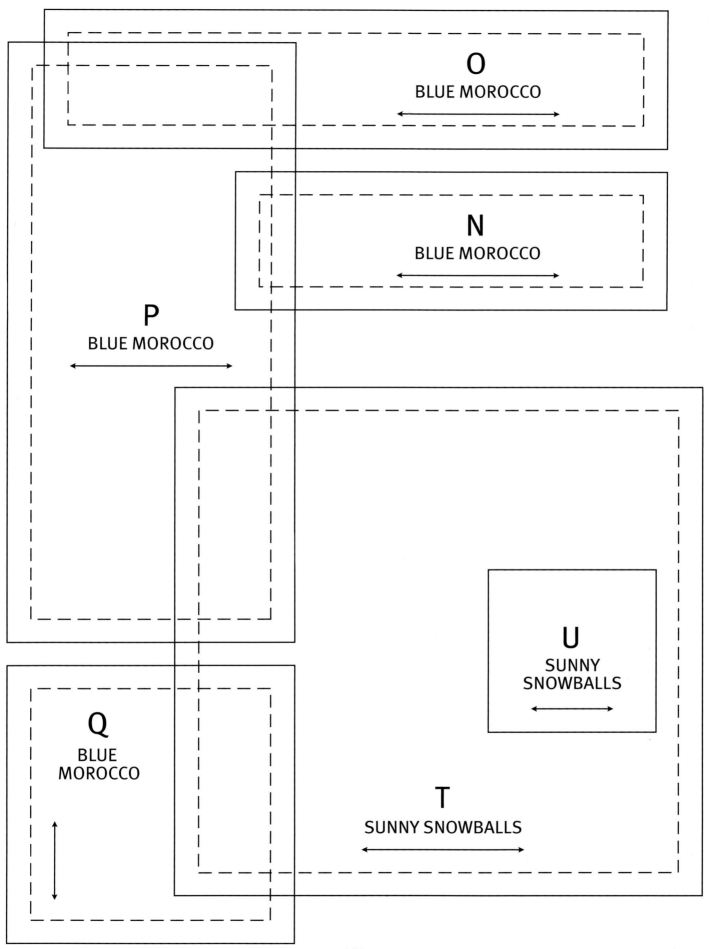

O
BLUE MOROCCO

N
BLUE MOROCCO

P
BLUE MOROCCO

U
SUNNY
SNOWBALLS

T
SUNNY SNOWBALLS

Q
BLUE
MOROCCO

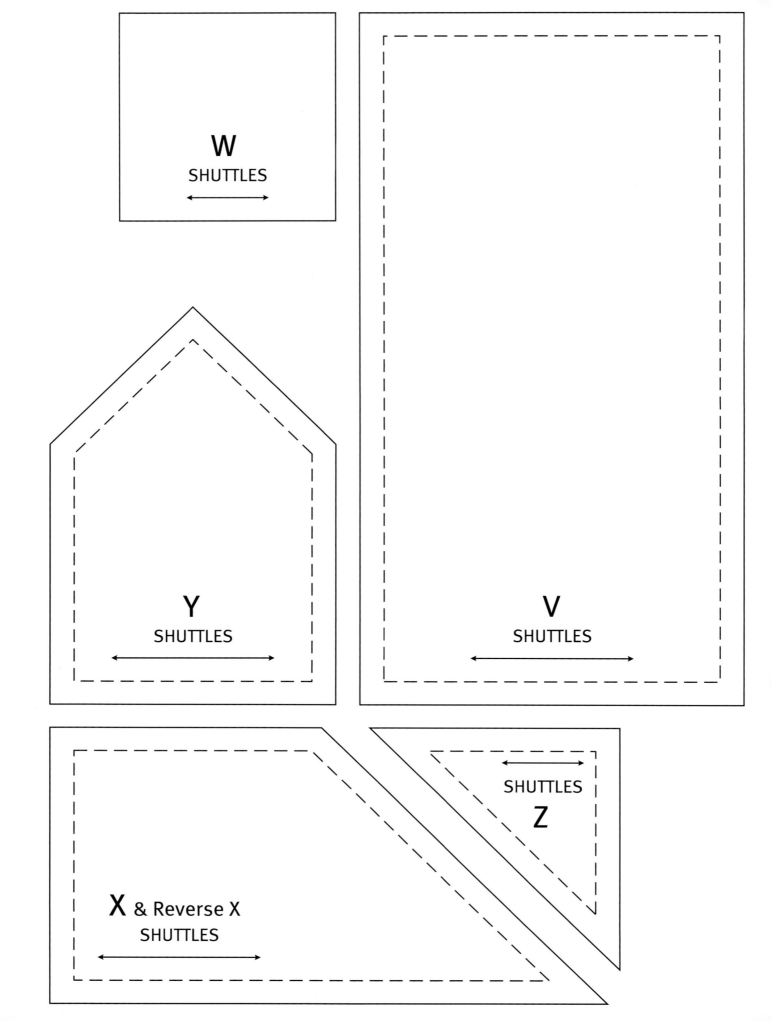

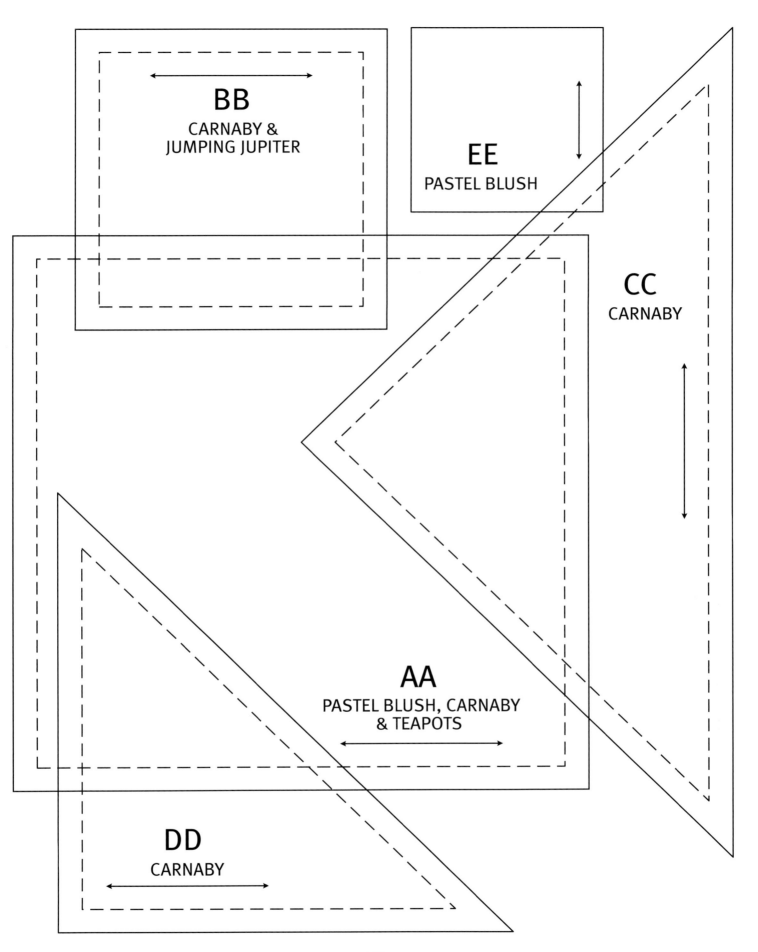

BB
CARNABY &
JUMPING JUPITER

EE
PASTEL BLUSH

CC
CARNABY

AA
PASTEL BLUSH, CARNABY
& TEAPOTS

DD
CARNABY

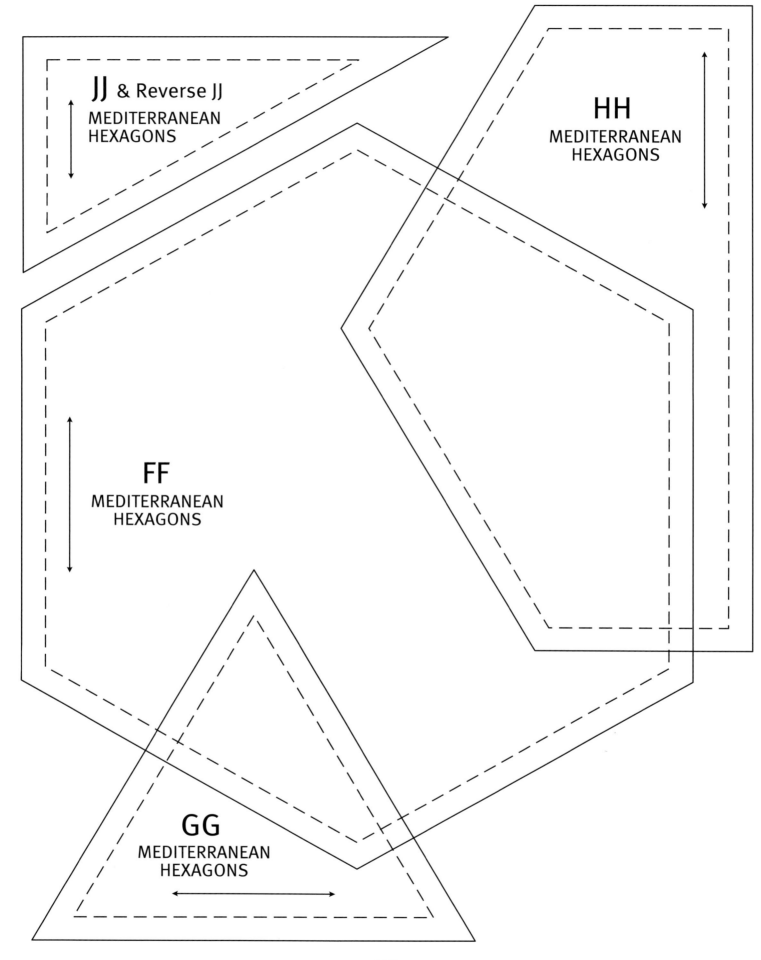

JJ & Reverse JJ
MEDITERRANEAN
HEXAGONS

HH
MEDITERRANEAN
HEXAGONS

FF
MEDITERRANEAN
HEXAGONS

GG
MEDITERRANEAN
HEXAGONS

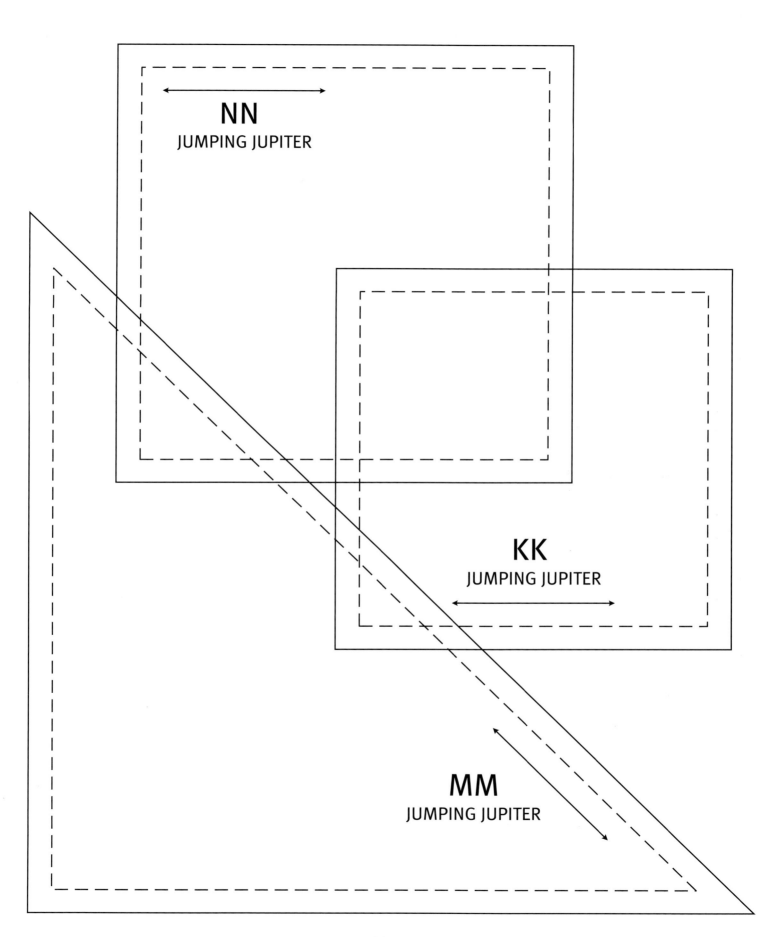

NN
JUMPING JUPITER

KK
JUMPING JUPITER

MM
JUMPING JUPITER

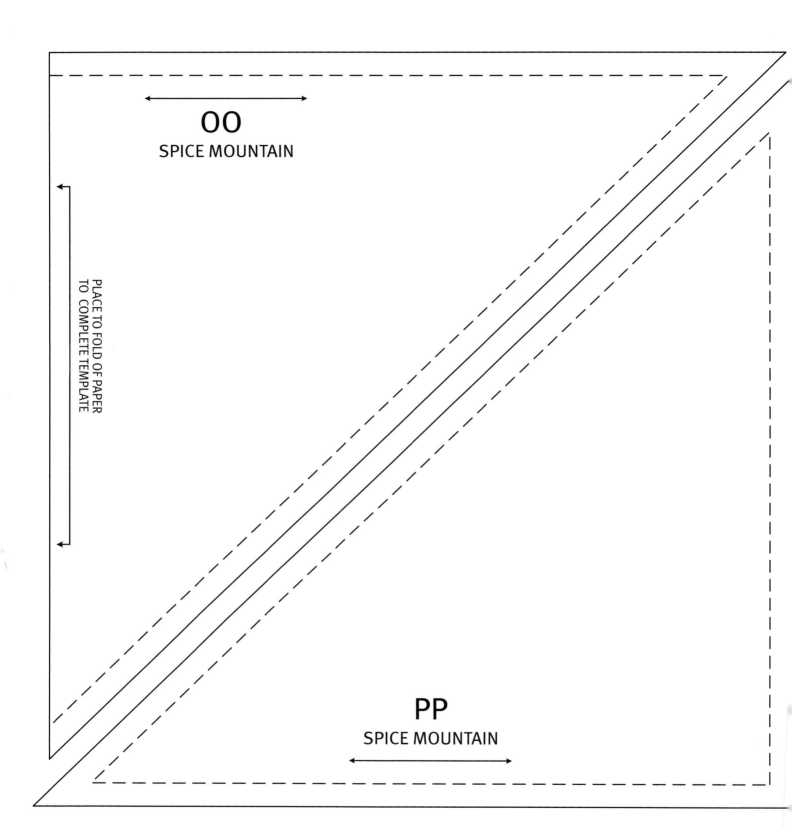

OO

SPICE MOUNTAIN

PLACE TO FOLD OF PAPER
TO COMPLETE TEMPLATE

PP

SPICE MOUNTAIN

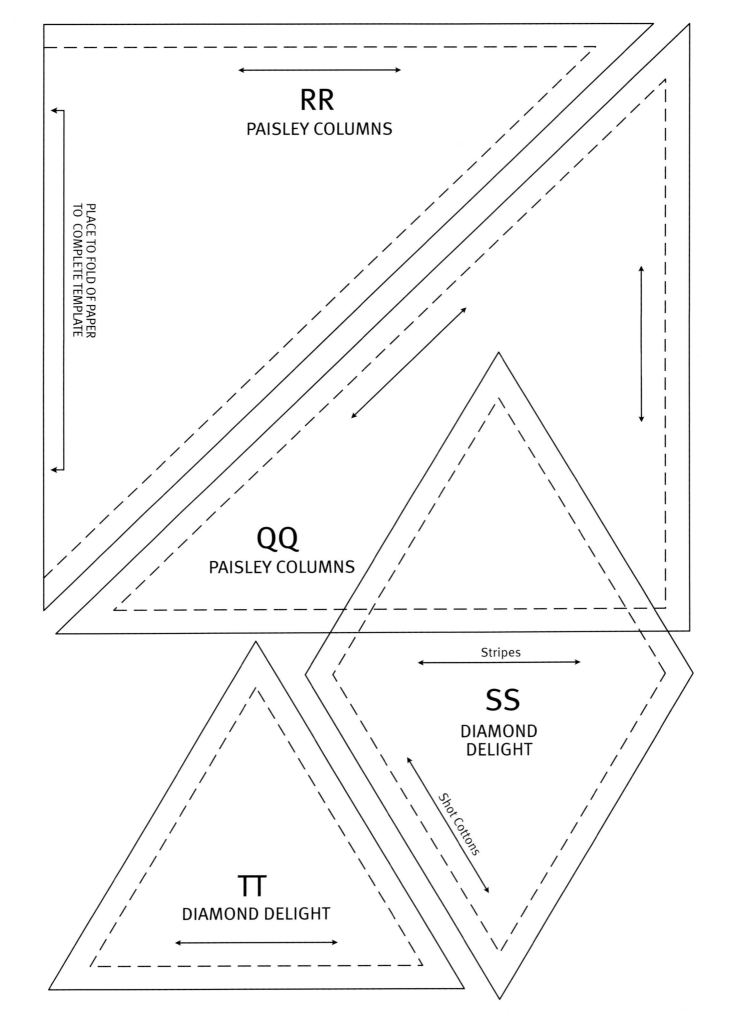

RR
PAISLEY COLUMNS

PLACE TO FOLD OF PAPER
TO COMPLETE TEMPLATE

QQ
PAISLEY COLUMNS

Stripes

SS
DIAMOND
DELIGHT

Shot Cottons

TT
DIAMOND DELIGHT

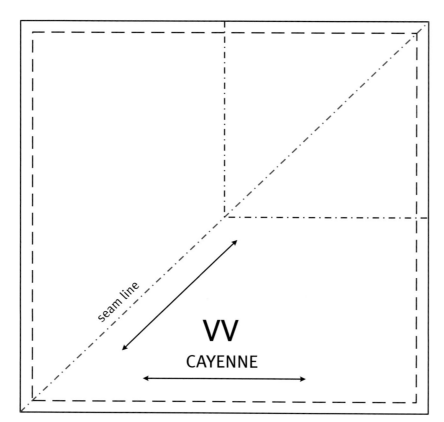

All the templates on this page are printed at 50% of real size. To use, scale up 200% on a photocopier.

VV
CAYENNE

seam line

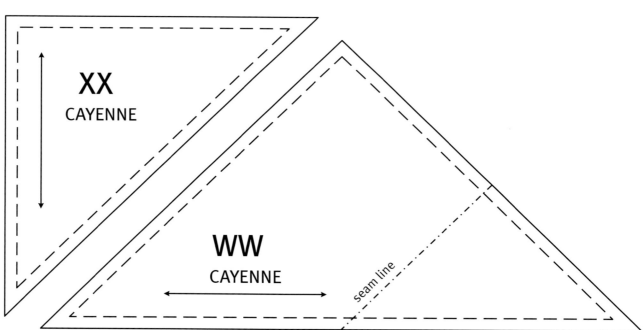

XX
CAYENNE

WW
CAYENNE

seam line

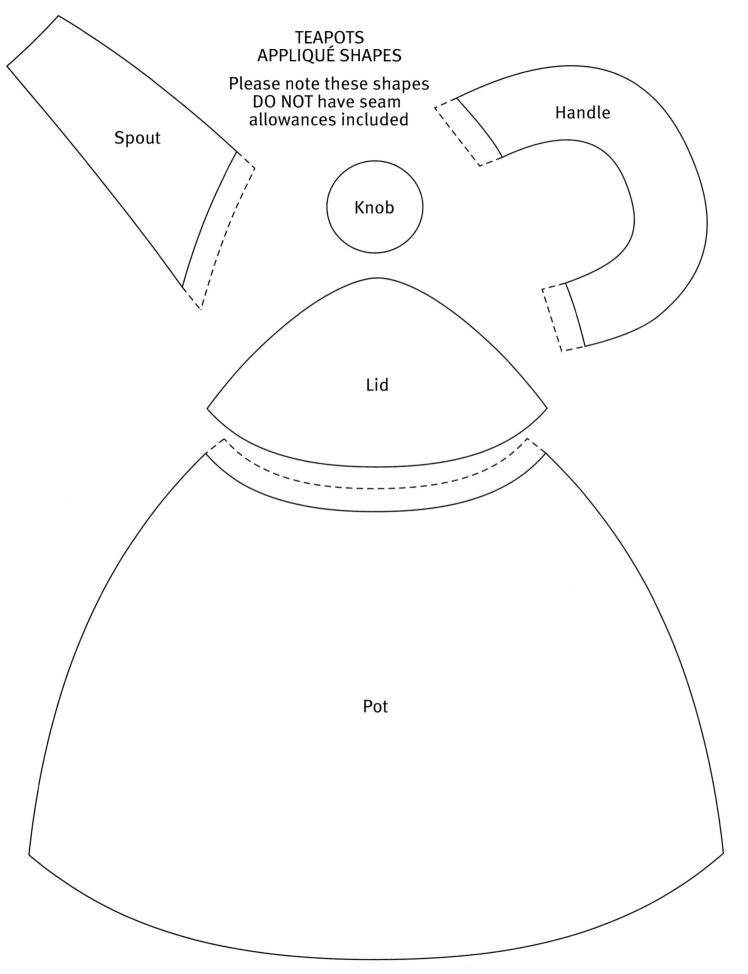

TEAPOTS
APPLIQUÉ SHAPES
Please note these shapes
DO NOT have seam
allowances included

Spout

Handle

Knob

Lid

Pot

patchwork know-how

These instructions are intended for the novice quilt maker, providing the basic information needed to make the projects in this book, along with some useful tips.

EXPERIENCE RATINGS
* Easy, straightforward, suitable for a beginner.
** Suitable for the average patchwork and quilter.
*** For the more experienced patchwork and quilter.

ABOUT THE FABRICS
The fabrics used for the quilts in this book are from Kaffe Fassett Collective. The first two letters of the fabric codes denote the designer:
GP is the code for the Kaffe Fassett collection
PJ is the code for the Philip Jacobs collection
BM is the code for the Brandon Mably collection.

PREPARING THE FABRIC
Prewash all new fabrics before you begin, to ensure that there will be no uneven shrinkage and no bleeding of colours when the finished quilt is laundered. Press the fabric whilst it is still damp to return crispness to it. All fabric requirements in this book are calculated on a 40in (101.5cm) usable fabric width, to allow for shrinkage and selvedge removal.

MAKING TEMPLATES
Transparent template plastic is the best material to use: it is durable and allows you to see the fabric and select certain motifs. You can also use thin stiff cardboard.

Templates for machine piecing
1 Trace off the actual–sized template provided either directly on to template plastic, or tracing paper, and then on to thin cardboard. Use a ruler to help you trace off the straight cutting line, dotted seam line and grain lines.
   Some of the templates in this book were too large to print complete. Transfer the template onto the fold of a large sheet of paper, cut out and open out for the full template.
2 Cut out the traced off template using a craft knife, a ruler and a self–healing cutting mat.
3 Punch holes in the corners of the template, at each point on the seam line, using a hole punch.

Templates for hand piecing
• Make a template as for machine piecing, but do not trace off the cutting line. Use the dotted seam line as the outer edge of the template.

• This template allows you to draw the seam lines directly on to the fabric. The seam allowances can then be cut by eye around the patch.

CUTTING THE FABRIC
On the individual instructions for each project, you will find a summary of all the patch shapes used.
   Always mark and cut out any border and binding strips first, followed by the largest patch shapes and finally the smallest ones, to make the most efficient use of your fabric. The border and binding strips are best cut using a rotary cutter.

Rotary cutting
Rotary cut strips are usually cut across the fabric from selvedge to selvedge, but some projects may vary, so please read through all the instructions before you start cutting the fabrics.

1 Before beginning to cut, press out any folds or creases in the fabric. If you are cutting a large piece of fabric, you will need to fold it several times to fit the cutting mat. When there is only a single fold, place the fold facing you. If the fabric is too wide to be folded only once, fold it concertina-style until it fits your mat. A small rotary cutter with a sharp blade will cut up to six layers of fabric; a large cutter up to eight layers.

2 To ensure that your cut strips are straight and even, the folds must be placed exactly parallel to the straight edges of the fabric and along a line on the cutting mat.

3 Place a plastic ruler over the raw edge of the fabric, overlapping it about ½in (1.25cm). Make sure that the ruler is at right angles to both the straight edges and the fold to ensure that you cut along the straight grain. Press down on the ruler and wheel the cutter away from you along the edge of the ruler.

4 Open out the fabric to check the edge. Don't worry if it's not perfectly straight – a little wiggle will not show when the quilt is stitched together. Re-fold fabric, then place the ruler over the trimmed edge, aligning the edge with the markings on the ruler that match the correct strip width. Cut strip along the edge of the ruler.

USING TEMPLATES
The most efficient way to cut out templates is by first rotary cutting a strip of fabric to the width stated for your template, and then marking off your templates along the strip, edge to edge at the required angle. This method leaves hardly any waste and gives a random effect to your patches.
   A less efficient method is to 'fussy cut' them, where the templates are cut individually by placing them on particular motifs or stripes, to create special effects. Although this method is more wasteful, it yields very interesting results.

1 Place the template face down, on the wrong side of the fabric, with the grain-line arrow following the straight grain of the fabric, if indicated. Be careful though – check with your individual instructions, as some instructions may ask you to cut patches on varying grains.

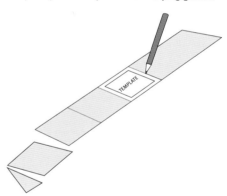

2 Hold the template firmly in place and draw around it with a sharp pencil or crayon, marking in the corner dots or seam lines. To save fabric, position patches close together or even touching. Don't worry if outlines positioned on the straight grain when drawn on striped fabrics do not always match the stripes when cut – this will add a degree of visual excitement to the patchwork!

3 Once you've drawn all the pieces needed, you are ready to cut the fabric, with either a rotary cutter and ruler or a pair of sharp sewing scissors.

BASIC HAND AND MACHINE PIECING
Patches can be stitched together by hand or machine. Machine stitching is quicker, but hand assembly allows you to carry your patches around with you and work on them in every spare moment. The choice is yours. For techniques that are new to you, practise on scrap pieces of fabric until you feel confident.

Machine piecing

Follow the quilt instructions for the order in which to piece the individual patchwork blocks and then assemble the blocks together in rows.

1 Seam lines are not marked on the fabric for simple shapes, so stitch ¼in (6mm) seams using the machine needle plate, a ¼in (6mm) wide machine foot, or tape stuck to the machine as a guide. Pin two patches with right sides together, matching edges.

For some shapes, particularly diamonds you need to match the sewing lines, not the fabric edges. Place 2 diamonds right sides together but offset so that the sewing lines intersect at the correct position. Use pins to secure for sewing.

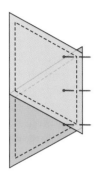

Set your machine at 10–12 stitches per inch (2.5cm) and stitch seams from edge to edge, removing pins as you feed the fabric through the machine.

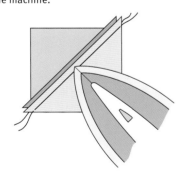

2 Press the seams of each patchwork block to one side before attempting to join it to another block. When joining diamond shaped blocks you will need to offset the blocks in the same way as diamond shaped patches, matching the sewing lines, not the fabric edges.

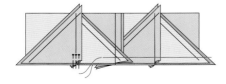

3 When joining rows of blocks, make sure that adjacent seam allowances are pressed in opposite directions to reduce bulk and make matching easier. Pin pieces together directly through the stitch line and to the right and left of the seam. Remove pins as you sew. Continue pressing seams to one side as you work.

Hand piecing

1 Pin two patches with right sides together, so that the marked seam lines are facing outwards.

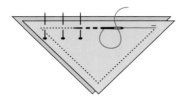

2 Using a single strand of strong thread, secure the corner of a seam line with a couple of back stitches.

3 Sew running stitches along the marked line, working 8–10 stitches per inch (2.5cm) and ending at the opposite seam line corner with a few back stitches. When hand piecing never stitch over the seam allowances.

4 Press the seams to one side, as shown in machine piecing (Step 2).

MACHINE APPLIQUÉ WITH ADHESIVE WEB

To make appliqué very easy you can use adhesive web (which comes attached to a paper backing sheet) to bond the motifs to the background fabric. There are two types of web available: the first keeps the pieces in place while they are stitched, the second permanently attaches the pieces so that no sewing is required. Follow steps 1 and 2 for the non-sew type and steps 1–3 for the type that requires sewing.

1 Trace the reversed appliqué design onto the paper side of the adhesive web leaving a ¼in (6mm) gap between all the shapes. Roughly cut out the motifs ⅛in (3mm) outside your drawn line.

2 Bond the motifs to the reverse of your chosen fabrics. Cut out on the drawn line with very sharp scissors. Remove the backing paper by scoring the centre of the motif carefully with a scissor point and peeling the paper away from the centre out (to prevent damage to the edges). Place the motifs onto the background, noting any which may be layered. Cover with a clean cloth and bond with a hot iron (check instructions for temperature setting as adhesive web can vary depending on the manufacturer).

3 Using a contrasting or toning coloured thread in your machine, work small close zigzag stitches (or a blanket stitch if your machine has one) around the edge of the motifs; the majority of the stitching should sit on the appliqué shape. When stitching up to points stop with the machine needle in the down position, lift the foot of your machine, pivot the work, lower the foot and continue to stitch. Make sure all the raw edges are stitched.

HAND APPLIQUÉ

Good preparation is essential for speedy and accurate hand appliqué. The finger-pressing method is suitable for needle-turning application, used for simple shapes like leaves and flowers. Using a card template is the best method for bold simple motifs such as circles.

Finger–pressing method

1 To make your template, transfer the appliqué design using carbon paper on to stiff card, and cut out the template. Trace around the outline of your appliquéd shape on to the right side of your fabric using a well sharpened pencil. Cut out shapes, adding by eye a ¼in (6mm) seam allowance all around.

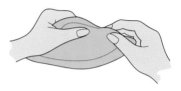

2 Hold shape right side up and fold under the seam, turning along your drawn line, pinch to form a crease. Dampening the fabric makes this very easy. When using shapes with 'points' such as leaves, turn in the seam allowance at the 'point' first, as shown in the diagram. Then continue all round the shape. If your shapes have sharp curves, you can snip the seam allowance to ease the curve. Take care not to stretch the appliqué shapes as you work.

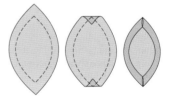

Card template method

1 Cut out appliqué shapes as shown in step 1 of finger-pressing. Make a circular template from thin cardboard, without seam allowances.

2 Using a matching thread, work a row of running stitches close to the edge of the fabric circle. Place a thin cardboard template in the centre of the fabric circle on the wrong side of the fabric.

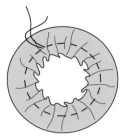

3 Carefully pull up the running stitches to gather up the edge of the fabric circle around the cardboard template. Press, so that no puckers or tucks appear on the right side. Then, carefully pop out the cardboard template without distorting the fabric shape.

Straight stems
Place fabric face down and simply press over the ¼in (6mm) seam allowance along each edge. You don't need to finish the ends of stems that are layered under other appliqué shapes. Where the end of the stem is visible, simply tuck under the end and finish neatly.

Needle-turning application
Take the appliqué shape and pin in position. Stroke the seam allowance under with the tip of the needle as far as the creased pencil line, and hold securely in place with your thumb. Using a matching thread, bring the needle up from the back of the block into the edge of the shape and proceed to blind-hem in place. (This stitch allows the motifs to appear to be held on invisibly.) To do this, bring the thread out from below through the folded edge of the motif, never on the top. The stitches must be small, even and close together to prevent the seam allowance from unfolding and from frayed edges appearing. Try to avoid pulling the stitches too tight, as this will cause the motifs to pucker up. Work around the whole shape, stroking under each small section before sewing.

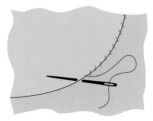

QUILTING
When you have finished piecing your patchwork and added any borders, press it carefully. It is now ready for quilting.

Marking quilting designs and motifs
Many tools are available for marking quilting patterns, check the manufacturer's instructions for use and test on scraps of fabric from your project. Use an acrylic ruler for marking straight lines.

Stencils
Some designs require stencils, these can be made at home, by transferring the designs on to template plastic, or stiff cardboard. The design is then cut away in the form of long dashes, to act as guides for both internal and external lines. These stencils are a quick method for producing an identical set of repeated designs.

Preparing the backing and batting
• Remove the selvedges and piece together the backing fabric to form a backing at least 4in (10cm) larger all round than the patchwork top.

• Choose a fairly thin batting, preferably pure cotton, to give your quilt a flat appearance. If your batting has been rolled up, unroll it and let it rest before cutting it to the same size as the backing.

• For a large quilt it may be necessary to join two pieces of batting to fit. Lay the pieces of batting on a flat surface so that they overlap by around 8in (20cm). Cut a curved line through both layers.

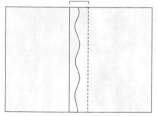
overlap wadding

• Carefully peel away the two narrow pieces and discard. Butt the curved cut edges back together. Stitch the two pieces together using a large herringbone stitch.

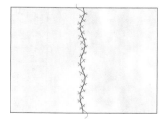

BASTING THE LAYERS TOGETHER
1 On the floor or on a large work surface, lay out the backing with wrong side uppermost. Use weights along the edges to keep it taut.

2 Lay the batting on the backing and smooth it out gently. Next lay the patchwork top, right side up, on top of the batting and smooth gently until there are no wrinkles. Pin at the corners and at the midpoints of each side, close to the edges.

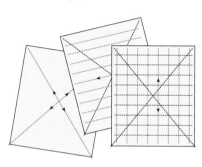

3 Beginning at the centre, baste diagonal lines outwards to the corners, making your stitches about 3in (7.5cm) long. Then, again starting at the centre, baste horizontal and vertical lines out to the edges. Continue basting until you have basted a grid of lines about 4in (10cm) apart over the entire quilt.

4 For speed, when machine quilting, some quilters prefer to baste their quilt sandwich layers together using rust-proof safety pins, spaced at 4in (10cm) intervals over the entire quilt.

HAND QUILTING
This is best done with the quilt mounted on a quilting frame or hoop, but as long as you have basted the quilt well, a frame is not essential. With the quilt top facing upwards, begin at the centre of the quilt and make even running stitches following the design. It is more important to make even stitches on both sides of the quilt than to make small ones. Start and finish your stitching with back stitches and bury the ends of your threads in the batting.

MACHINE QUILTING

• For a flat looking quilt, always use a walking foot on your machine for stitching straight lines, and a darning foot for free–motion quilting.

• It is best to start your quilting at the centre of the quilt and work out towards the borders, doing the straight quilting lines first (stitch-in-the-ditch) followed by the free-motion quilting.

• When free motion-quilting stitch in a loose meandering style as shown in the diagrams. Do not stitch too closely as this will make the quilt feel stiff when finished. If you wish you can include floral themes or follow shapes on the printed fabrics for added interest.

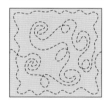

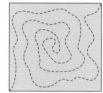

• Make it easier for yourself by handling the quilt properly. Roll up the excess quilt neatly to fit under your sewing machine arm, and use a table or chair to help support the weight of the quilt that hangs down the other side.

FINISHING

Preparing to bind the edges
Once you have quilted or tied your quilt sandwich together, remove all the basting stitches. Then, baste around the outer edge of the quilt ¼in (6mm) from the edge of the top patchwork layer. Trim the back and batting to the edge of the patchwork and straighten the edge of the patchwork if necessary.

Making the binding
1 Cut bias or straight grain strips the width required for your binding, making sure the grain-line is running the correct way on your straight grain strips. Cut enough strips until you have the required length to go around the edge of your quilt.

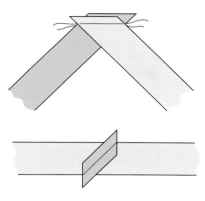

2 To join strips together, the two ends that are to be joined must be cut at a 45 degree angle, as above. Stitch right sides together, trim turnings and press seam open.

Binding the edges

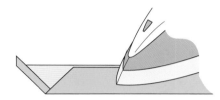

1 Cut the starting end of binding strip at a 45 degree angle, fold a ¼in (6mm) turning to wrong side along cut edge and press in place. With wrong sides together, fold strip in half lengthways, keeping raw edges level, and press.

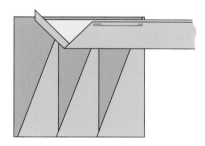

2 Starting at the centre of one of the long edges, place the doubled binding on to the right side of the quilt keeping raw edges level. Stitch the binding in place starting ¼in (6mm) in from the diagonal folded edge. Reverse stitch to secure, and work ¼in (6mm) in from edge of the quilt towards first corner of quilt. Stop ¼in (6mm) in from corner and work a few reverse stitches.

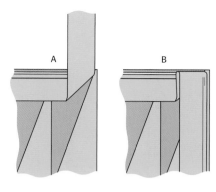

3 Fold the loose end of the binding up, making a 45 degree angle (see A). Keeping the diagonal fold in place, fold the binding back down, aligning the raw edges with the next side of the quilt. Starting at the point where the last stitch ended, stitch down the next side (see B).

4 Continue to stitch the binding in place around all the quilt edges in this way, tucking the finishing end of the binding inside the diagonal starting section.

5 Turn the folded edge of the binding on to the back of the quilt. Hand stitch the folded edge in place just covering binding machine stitches, and folding a mitre at each corner

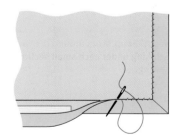

glossary of terms

Adhesive or fusible web This comes attached to a paper backing sheet and is used to bond appliqué motifs to a background fabric. There are 2 types of web available, the first keeps the pieces in place whilst they are stitched, the second permanently attaches the pieces so that no sewing is required.

Appliqué The technique of stitching fabric shapes on to a background to create a design. It can be applied either by hand or machine with a decorative embroidery stitch, such as buttonhole, or satin stitch.

Backing The bottom layer of a quilt sandwich. It is made of fabric pieced to the size of the quilt top with the addition of about 4in (10.25cm) all around to allow for quilting take-up.

Basting or tacking This is a means of holding two fabric layers or the layers of a quilt sandwich together temporarily with large hand stitches, or pins.

Batting or wadding This is the middle layer, or padding in a quilt. It can be made of cotton, wool, silk or synthetic fibres.

Bias The diagonal grain of a fabric. This is the direction which has the most give or stretch, making it ideal for bindings, especially on curved edges.

Binding A narrow strip of fabric used to finish off the edges of quilts or projects; it can be cut on the straight grain of a fabric or on the bias.

Block A single design unit that when stitched together with other blocks create the quilt top. It is most often a square, hexagon, or rectangle, but it can be any shape. It can be pieced or plain.

Border A frame of fabric stitched to the outer edges of the quilt top. Borders can be narrow or wide, pieced or plain. As well as making the quilt larger, they unify the overall design and draw attention to the central area.

Chalk pencils Available in various colours, they are used for marking lines, or spots on fabric.

Cutting mat Designed for use with a rotary cutter, it is made from a special 'self-healing' material that keeps your cutting blade sharp. Cutting mats come in various sizes and are usually marked with a grid to help you line up the edges of fabric and cut out larger pieces.

Design wall Used for laying out fabric patches before sewing. A large wall or folding board covered with flannel fabric or cotton batting in a neutral shade (dull beige or grey work well) will hold fabric in place so that an overall view can be taken of the placement.

Free-motion quilting Curved wavy quilting lines stitched in a random manner. Stitching diagrams are often given for you to follow as a loose guide.

Fussy cutting This is when a template is placed on a particular motif, or stripe, to obtain interesting effects. This method is not as efficient as strip cutting, but yields very interesting results.

Grain The direction in which the threads run in a woven fabric. In a vertical direction it is called the lengthwise grain, which has very little stretch. The horizontal direction, or crosswise grain is slightly stretchy, but diagonally the fabric has a lot of stretch. This grain is called the bias. Wherever possible the grain of a fabric should run in the same direction on a quilt block and borders.

Grain lines These are arrows printed on templates which should be aligned with the fabric grain.

Inset seams or setting-in A patchwork technique whereby one patch (or block) is stitched into a 'V' shape formed by the joining of two other patches (or blocks).

Patch A small shaped piece of fabric used in the making of a patchwork pattern.

Patchwork The technique of stitching small pieces of fabric (patches) together to create a larger piece of fabric, usually forming a design.

Pieced quilt A quilt composed of patches.

Quilting Traditionally done by hand with running stitches, but for speed modern quilts are often stitched by machine. The stitches are sewn through the top, wadding and backing to hold the three layers together. Quilting stitches are usually worked in some form of design, but they can be random.

Quilting hoop Consists of two wooden circular or oval rings with a screw adjuster on the outer ring. It stabilises the quilt layers, helping to create an even tension.

Reducing Glass Used for viewing the complete composition of a quilt at a glance. It works like a magnifier in reverse. A useful tool for checking fabric placement before piecing a quilt.

Rotary cutter A sharp circular blade attached to a handle for quick, accurate cutting. It is a device that can be used to cut several layers of fabric at one time. It must be used in conjunction with a 'self-healing' cutting mat and a thick plastic ruler.

Rotary ruler A thick, clear plastic ruler marked with lines in imperial or metric measurements. Sometimes they also have diagonal lines indicating 45 and 60 degree angles. A rotary ruler is used as a guide when cutting out fabric pieces using a rotary cutter.

Sashing A piece or pieced sections of fabric interspaced between blocks.

Sashing posts When blocks have sashing between them the corner squares are known as sashing posts.

Selvedges Also known as selvages, these are the firmly woven edges down each side of a fabric length. Selvedges should be trimmed off before cutting out your fabric, as they are more liable to shrink when the fabric is washed.

Stitch-in-the-ditch or Ditch quilting Also known as quilting-in-the-ditch. The quilting stitches are worked along the actual seam lines, to give a pieced quilt texture.

Template A pattern piece used as a guide for marking and cutting out fabric patches, or marking a quilting, or appliqué design. Usually made from plastic or strong card that can be reused many times. Templates for cutting fabric usually have marked grain lines which should be aligned with the fabric grain.

Threads One hundred percent cotton or cotton-covered polyester is best for hand and machine piecing. Choose a colour that matches your fabric. When sewing different colours and patterns together, choose a medium to light neutral colour, such as grey or ecru. Specialist quilting threads are available for hand and machine quilting.

Walking foot or Quilting foot This is a sewing machine foot with dual feed control. It is very helpful when quilting, as the fabric layers are fed evenly from the top and below, reducing the risk of slippage and puckering.

Yo-Yos A circle of fabric double the size of the finished puff is gathered up into a rosette shape.

ACKNOWLEDGMENTS

We are very grateful for the generosity and support of Robert Johnstone of Riad Idrissy and The Ruined Gardens (www.riadidrissy.com) for his bountiful hospitality and the introduction to David Amster, who has made Fez his home for the past 15 years and who gave us access to his carefully restored seventeenth-century home.

Also to Michel Biehn and his son, Paul, for the use of their beautifully decorated rooms and the garden of Café Fez at Le Jardin des Biehn (www.jardindesbiehn.com/en/).

A big thank you, too, to young artist and student Mustapha Harouni who acted as our local guide.

The fabric collection can be viewed online at
www.coatscrafts.co.uk *and* www.westminsterfabrics.com

Rowan 100% cotton premium thread, Anchor embroidery thread, and Prym sewing aids, distributed by Coats Crafts UK, Green Lane Mill, Holmfirth, West Yorkshire, HD9 2DX.
Tel: +44 (0) 1484 681881 • Fax: +44 (0) 1484 687920

Rowan 100% cotton premium thread and Anchor embroidery thread distributed in the USA by Westminster Fibers, 3430 Toringdon Way, Charlotte, North Carolina 28277.
Tel: 704 329 5800 • Fax: 704 329 5027

Prym productions distributed in the USA by
Prym-Dritz Corp, 950 Brisack Road, Spartanburg, SC 29303.
Tel: +1 864 576 5050 • Fax: +1 864 587 3353
email: pdmar@teleplex.net

OTHER TAUNTON TITLES AVAILABLE
Kaffe Fassett's *Quilt Romance*
Kaffe Fassett's *Quilts en Provence*
Kaffe Fassett's *Quilts in Sweden*
Kaffe Quilts Again
Kaffe Fassett's *Quilt Grandeur*

To place an order or to
request a catalog, contact

The Taunton Press, Inc.
63 South Main Street, P.O. Box 5506
Newtown, CT 06470-5506

www.taunton.com

Rowan/Coats Crafts UK, Green Lane Mill, Holmfirth,
West Yorkshire HD9 2DX, England.
Tel: +44 (0) 1484 681881 • Email: ccuk.sales@coats.com
www.coatscrafts.co.uk • www.knitrowan.co.uk

Westminster Lifestyle Fabrics, 3430 Toringdon Way, Suite 301,
Charlotte, NC, U.S.A
Tel: 704-329-5800 • Email: fabric@westminsterfibers.com
www.westminsterfabrics.com

distributors and stockists

Distributors of Rowan fabrics

AUSTRALIA
Australian Country Spinners, Pty Ltd,
Level 7, 409 St. Kilda Road,
Melbourne Vic 3004.
Tel: 03 9380 3888
Email: customerservice@auspinners.
com.au

AUSTRIA
Coats Harlander Ges.m.b.H
Autokaderstraße 29, 1210 Wien
Tel.: 00800 26272800
Email: coats.harlander@coats.com
www.coatscrafts.at

BELGIUM
Coats N.V., c/o Coats GmbH Kaiserstr.1
79341 Kenzingen, Germany
Tel: 0032 (0) 800 77 89 2
Email: sales.coatsninove@coats.com
www.coatscrafts.be

BULGARIA
Coats Bulgaria, 7 Magnaurska Shkola
Str., BG-1784 Sofia, Bulgaria
Tel: (+359 2) 976 77 41
Email: officebg@coats.com
www.coatsbulgaria.bg

CANADA
Westminster Fibers, 10 Roybridge Gate,
Suite 200, Vaughan, Ontario L4H 3M8
Tel: (800) 263-2354
Email: info@westminsterfibers.com

CHINA
Coats Shanghai Ltd, No 9 Building ,
Baosheng Road, Songjiang Industrial
Zone, Shanghai.
Tel: (86-21) 13816681825
Email: victor.li@coats.com

CYPRUS
Coats Bulgaria, 7 Magnaurska Shkola
Str., BG-1784 Sofia, Bulgaria
Tel: (+359 2) 976 77 41
Email: officebg@coats.com
www.coatscrafts.com.cy

CZECH REPUBLIC
Coats Czecho s.r.o.
Staré Mesto 246 569 32
Tel: (420) 461616633
Email: galanterie@coats.com
www.coatscrafts.cz

DENMARK
Carl J. Permin A/S Egegaardsvej
28 DK-2610 Rødovre
Tel: (45) 36 72 12 00
E-mail: permin@permin.dk

ESTONIA
Coats Eesti As
Ampri tee 9/4, 74011 Vlimsi Vald,
Harjumaa
Tel: +372 630 6252
Email: info@coats.ee
www.coatscrafts.co.ee

FINLAND
Coats Opti Crafts Oy
Huhtimontie 6, 04220 Kerava
Tel: 358-9-274871
Email: coatsopti.sales@coats.com
www.coatscrafts.fi

FRANCE
Coats France
c/o Coats GmbH, Kaiserstr. 1
79341 Kenzingen, Germany
Tel: 0810 060002
Email: artsdufil@coats.com
www.coatscrafts.fr

GERMANY
Coats GmbH
Kaiserstraße 1, 79341 Kenzingen
Tel: 0049 7644 802222
Email: kenzingen.vertrieb@coats.com
www.coatsgmbh.de

GREECE
Coats Bulgaria, 7 Magnaurska Shkola Str.,
BG-1784 Sofia, Bulgaria
Tel: (+359 2) 976 77 41
Email: officebg@coats.com
www.coatscrafts.gr

HOLLAND
Coats B.V., c/o Coats GmbH, Kaiserstr.1,
79341 Kenzingen, Germany
Tel: 0031 (0) 800 02 26 6488
Email: sales.coatsninove@coats.com
www.coatscrafts.be

HONG KONG
East Unity Company Ltd, Unit B2, 7/F.,
Block B, Kailey Industrial Centre,
12 Fung Yip Street, Chai Wan
Tel: (852) 2869 7110
Email: eastunityco@yahoo.com.hk

ICELAND
Storkurinn, Laugavegi 59, 101 Reykjavik
Tel: (354) 551 8258
Email: storkurinn@simnet.is

ITALY
Coats Cucirini Srl
Viale Sarca 223, 20126 Milano
Tel: 02 63615224
www.coatscucirini.com

KOREA
Coats Korea Co. Ltd, 5F Eyeon B/D,
935-40 Bangbae-Dong, 137-060
Tel: (82) 2 521 6262
Email: rozenpark@coats.com

LATVIA
Coats Latvija SIA
Mükusalas str. 41 b
Rïga LV-1004
Tel: +371 67 625173
Email: info.latvia@coats.com
www.coatscrafts.lv

LEBANON
y.knot, Saifi Village,
Mkhalissiya Street 162, Beirut
Tel: (961) 1 992211
Email: y.knot@cyberia.net.lb

LITHUANIA & RUSSIA
Coats Lietuva UAB, A. Juozapaviciaus
str. 6/2, LT-09310 Vilnius
Tel: +370 527 30971
Email: info@coats.lt
www.coatscrafts.lt

LUXEMBOURG
Coats N.V., c/o Coats GmbH,
Kaiserstr.1, 79341 Kenzingen,
Germany
Tel: 00 49 7644 802 222
Email: sales.coatsninove@coats.com
www.coatscrafts.be

MALTA
John Gregory Ltd, 8 Ta'Xbiex Sea Front,
Msida MSD 1512
Tel: +356 2133 0202
Email: raygreg@onvol.net

MEXICO
Estambres Crochet SA de CV,
Aaron Saenz 1891-7, PO Box
Santamaria, 64650 Monterrey
Tel: +52 (81) 8335-3870

NEW ZEALAND
ACS New Zealand, P.O Box 76199,
Northwood, Christchurch
Tel: 64 3 323 6665
Email: lynn@impactmg.co.nz

NORWAY
Falk Knappehuset AS,
Svinesundsveien 347, 1788 Halden
Tel: +47 555 393 00
Email: post@falkgruppen.no

PORTUGAL
Coats & Clark, Quinta de Cravel,
Apartado 444, 4431-968 Portugal
Tel: 00 351 223 770700

SINGAPORE
Golden Dragon Store, 101 Upper Cross
Street #02-51, People's Park Centre,
Singapore 058357
Tel: (65) 6 5358454
Email: gdscraft@hotmail.com

SLOVAKIA
Coats s.r.o.
Kopcianska 9485101 Bratislava
Tel: (421) 263532314
Email: galanteria@coats.com
www.coatscrafts.sk

SOUTH AFRICA
Arthur Bales Ltd
62 4th Avenue
Linden 2195
Tel: (27) 11 888 2401
Email: arthurb@new.co.za

SPAIN
Coats Fabra SAU, Avda Meridiana 350,
pta 13, 08027 Barcelona
Tel: (34) 932908400
Email: atencion.clientes@coats.com
www.coatscrafts.es

SWEDEN
Bröderna Falk Sybehör & Garn Engros,
Stationsvägen 2, 516 31 Dalsjöfors
Tel: (46) 40-6084002
Email: kundtjanst@falk.se

SWITZERLAND
Coats Stroppel AG
Stroppelstrasse 20
5417 Untersiggenthal
Tel: 00800 26272800
Email: coats.stroppel@coats.com
www.coatscrafts.ch

TAIWAN
Cactus Quality Co Ltd, 7FL-2, No. 140,
Sec.2 Roosevelt Rd, Taipei, 10084
Taiwan, R.O.C.
Tel: 00886-2-23656527
Email: cqcl@ms17.hinet.net

THAILAND
Global Wide Trading,
10 Lad Prao Soi 88, Bangkok 10310
Tel: 00 662 933 9019
Email: global.wide@yahoo.com

UK
Rowan
Green Lane Mill
Holmfirth
West Yorkshire
HD9 2DX
Tel: 01484 681881
Email: ccuk.sales@coats.com
www.knitrowan.co.uk

U.S.A
Westminster Fibers, 8 Shelter Drive,
Greer, South Carolina, 29650
Tel: (800) 445-9276
Email: info@westminsterfibers.com
www.westminsterfibers.com

For stockists in all other countries
please contact Rowan for details